Apples of Gold

Words "Fitly Spoken" from The Berean Call

A 366-Day Devotional Calendar

The Berean Call

Bend • Oregon

APPLES OF GOLD

Published by The Berean Call

ISBN 978-1-928660-73-6

Unless otherwise indicated, Scripture quotations are from
The Holy Bible, King James Version (KJV)

The Berean Call
PO Box 7019
Bend, Oregon, 97708-7019

PRINTED IN THE UNITED STATES OF AMERICA

To:

From:

January

January 1

The Bible is the unique revelation of God to mankind. It goes into great detail to support what it says, giving much evidence from prophecies fulfilled, from history, and from the accounts of eyewitnesses. It does not argue, however, nor support with further evidence, that which creation declares and makes self-evident to all mankind. It begins with the simple statement that God created the heavens and the earth, and then goes on from there. –TBC

The heavens declare the glory of God; and the firmament sheweth his handywork.

—Psalm 19:1

January 2

The perceived differences between the God of the Old Testament and the God of the New Testament are mainly the result of the presumptions we bring to the Scriptures rather than a natural interpretation of the same. For example, we see God's grace and mercy extended to Rahab and her family, even though her origin would forever preclude her entry into the nation of Israel. The same can be stated of Ruth the Moabitess. Indeed, the Old Testament Scriptures are full of examples of God acting in grace—overriding His pronouncements and showing His mercy. –TBC

And Joshua saved Rahab the harlot alive, and her father's household, and all that she had; and she dwelleth in Israel even unto this day; because she hid the messengers, which Joshua sent to spy out Jericho.

—JOSHUA 6:25

January 3

The way to search the real truth is to know the One who is truth, and to know what He has said and done. Draw near to God, and He will draw near to you. –TBC

He is the Rock, his work is perfect: for all his ways are judgment: a God of truth and without iniquity, just and right is he.

—DEUTERONOMY 32:4

January 4

God shows no partiality to people. Throughout the Scriptures we see examples of His graciousness to many who were not of the household of Israel. Ruth, Rahab, and Naaman are but a few examples. Jesus stated very clearly that when all is done with He would only have "one fold" (flock) of sheep. Going back to Galatians 3:28, "There is neither Jew nor Greek, there is neither bond nor free, there is neither male nor female: for ye are all one in Christ Jesus." May God encourage us in this. –TBC

And other sheep I have, which are not of this fold:
them also I must bring, and they shall hear my voice;
and there shall be one fold, and one shepherd.

—JOHN 10:16

January 5

There are quite a number of occasions when the Lord exhibited awareness beyond human ability. Prior to his arrival at Bethany, He knew that Lazarus was dead. He foresaw the destruction and ruin of Jerusalem. He told Peter where a fish could be obtained that had a coin in its mouth. Time and again, He looked into the "hearts" of people such as the rich young ruler and put His finger squarely upon the issue that concerned them and that they would not name. –TBC

Then Jesus beholding him loved him, and said unto him, One thing thou lackest: go thy way, sell whatsoever thou hast, and give to the poor, and thou shalt have treasure in heaven: and come, take up the cross, and follow me.

—MARK 10:21

January 6

Man has no demands that he can make upon God. We cannot demand that He save us. We cannot appeal to some right to be saved. Granted, we cannot come to Christ except the Father draw us. Yet we must consent, and that consent must be a genuine choice or it is all a sham! –TBC

This is the law of him in whom is the plague of leprosy, whose hand is not able to get that which pertaineth to his cleansing.

—LEVITICUS 14:32

January 7

Have you ever received Jesus Christ as your Lord and Savior, believed that He died for your sins upon the Cross, and rose again the third day? Confess your sins and ask Christ to come into your heart. Then you will have the victory over Satan because Christ, who comes to dwell in your heart by faith, is greater than Satan. That doesn't mean that Satan cannot tempt or attack you, since he did that to Christ Himself when He walked this earth. But it does mean that you can resist the devil and he will flee from you. –TBC

If we confess our sins, he is faithful and just to forgive us our sins, and to cleanse us from all unrighteousness.

—1 JOHN 1:9

January 8

Even the Old Testament sacrificial system prefigured salvation by faith alone. Speaking of the priestly garments, Ezekiel wrote that "they shall have linen bonnets upon their heads…linen breeches upon their loins; they shall not gird themselves with any thing that causeth sweat" (Ezekiel 44:18). Man was to "earn" his living by "the sweat of thy face…" (Genesis 3:19). But nothing that involves "work" will "earn" you salvation. –TBC

But to him that worketh not, but believeth on him that justifieth the ungodly, his faith is counted for righteousness.

—ROMANS 4:5

January 9

Did God in the Old Testament ever suggest that Israel be open to hear and see the "ray of light" among the Baal worshipers; or Jesus in the New Testament or Paul or Peter suggest that there is truth in all religions? Indeed not! –TBC

And Nadab and Abihu died, when they offered strange fire before the LORD.

—NUMBERS 26:61

January 10

If you know Jesus Christ as your personal Savior, and if you spend time daily reading the Bible and in prayer, God can answer all your questions—but not all at once. The Holy Spirit will lead us into all truth, which sets us free…from fear, from every bondage. When we are obedient to that which we already know God has taught us, it's amazing how He provides new insight about things we have not understood. –TBC

Thy word have I hid in mine heart,
that I might not sin against thee.

—Psalm 119:11

January 11

If you really love someone, you don't want to see them continue in false beliefs. It would be much easier for us to remain silent, but one day we must give an account to the Lord, and we don't want to be rebuked by Him because we didn't speak the truth. –TBC

Faithful are the wounds of a friend; but the kisses of an enemy are deceitful.

—PROVERBS 27:6

January 12

The fear of man, or a desire to be well thought of by others, or to gain some important or influential person's approval, has led many astray. We need to remember that one day we will give an account to Him. Time is so very short and eternity so long! —TBC

The fear of man bringeth a snare: but whoso putteth his trust in the LORD shall be safe.

—PROVERBS 29:25

January 13

Can you still be saved if your faith is weak? Do we ever come to a point in our life when we think our faith is strong? Our relationship with the Lord Jesus Christ is not predicated upon our strength; it is based upon what a God "that cannot lie" (Titus 1:2) has promised. The difficult part is getting our eyes off our own weaknesses, our past record of failures, and being willing to step out in faith. That's why it's so important to prayerfully read His Word daily. —TBC

And Jesus said unto them, Because of your unbelief: for verily I say unto you, If ye have faith as a grain of mustard seed, ye shall say unto this mountain, Remove hence to yonder place; and it shall remove; and nothing shall be impossible unto you.

—MATTHEW 17:20

January 14

David and the other authors of the Psalms were very human individuals who experienced all the failures, shortcomings, fears, and trouble that we still face today. Nevertheless, they stepped out and, as a consequence, saw the Lord answer prayer, deliver them from tremendous difficulties, and protect them from great peril. This gave them a "track record" that they took with them for the rest of their life. –TBC

He brought me up also out of an horrible pit, out of the miry clay, and set my feet upon a rock, and established my goings.

—Psalm 40:2

January 15

The solution to, and protection from, mind interference in any form is to submit one's will and mind to Christ. This begins by being born again and continues as we walk in submission to His will and His ways. –TBC

Thou wilt keep him in perfect peace, whose mind is stayed on thee: because he trusteth in thee.

—ISAIAH 26:3

January 16

The word "love" has certainly lost much meaning, particularly in our own culture, where it seems to be little more than an emotional feeling that comes and goes. The Lord spoke much of love and noted that His disciples would be recognized by the love they had for one another (John 13:34-35). John asked how any man could say he loves God whom he cannot see when he cannot love his brother whom he does see (I John 4:20). Love is much more than an emotion dependent upon feelings. God does command us to love everyone, something we cannot do in our own strength when there are so many who appear to be "unlovable." –TBC

A new commandment I give unto you, That ye love one another; as I have loved you, that ye also love one another.

—John 13:34

January 17

Granted, the Lord has called us to be stewards and has entrusted certain items and responsibilities into our hands (Matthew 25:14–29; Luke 12:42), but as the scripture below notes, it is the Lord who is truly doing the keeping. This agrees with Psalm 34:7, "The angel of the Lord encampeth round about them that fear him, and delivereth them." –TBC

Except the LORD build the house,
they labour in vain that build it:
except the LORD keep the city,
the watchman waketh but in vain.

—PSALM 127:1

January 18

While the contemporary scene may sometimes dismay us and be cause for fervent prayer, it is also a call to Bereanship and personal diligence in scriptural study, prayer, and obedience to those things we do understand from God's Word, for therein lies growth in discernment. Through it all, we can find the Lord giving us opportunity and challenge for growth as well as intercessory service and the ability to admonish each other daily. –TBC

And such as do wickedly against the covenant shall be corrupt by flatteries: but the people that do know their God shall be strong, and do exploits.

—DANIEL 11:32

January 19

Focusing on man is the path to discouragement. Jeremiah 17:5 tells us that "cursed be the man that trusteth in man, and maketh flesh his arm, and whose heart departeth from the Lord." One of our adversary's strategies is to wear down believers (Galatians 6:9; 1 Peter 5:8). The apostle Paul urges us to run this race (and a race is certainly wearying), "looking unto Jesus, the author and finisher of our faith..." (Hebrews 12:2). –TBC

And let us not be weary in well-doing: for in due season we shall reap, if we faint not.

—GALATIANS 6:9

January 20

The peace of Jerusalem for which we are to pray is that which the Bible promises will come when the Prince of Peace has returned (Isaiah 9:6). Until then, despite all human efforts to obtain it or to destroy it, true peace will never come to Jerusalem. The peace that passes understanding, which God gives every true believer, is just a tiny foretaste of this true peace. –TBC

For unto us a child is born, unto us a son is given: and the government shall be upon his shoulder: and his name shall be called Wonderful, Counsellor, The mighty God, The everlasting Father, The Prince of Peace.

—Isaiah 9:6

January 21

Many Roman emperors declared themselves deity and demanded for themselves an "honor" from men that could only be accorded to God. The honor Paul instructed us to give to widows is different. Here he is speaking of the physical support a congregation is obligated to give to a widow who has no immediate family to support her. We are also to honor our parents and those in authority. But this has nothing to do with the honor demanded by despots throughout history. That kind of honor we can only give to God. –TBC

But Peter took him up, saying,
Stand up; I myself am a man.

—ACTS 10:26

January 22

Consider the language employed today in society compared with that of the Jews, who regarded the name of God as so holy that they would not dare even to write or pronounce it. Modern Americans see no problem in using it as an adjective to emphasize a statement. It is used as a punch line in sitcoms. It is no longer revered. That being said, is our goal to force an outward conformity on people, or, through the demonstration of our lives and our words, do we faithfully preach the Gospel so that they may be changed from the inside out? The words of a person are but symptoms—and the Great Physician does not treat just symptoms, but rather seeks to cure the root problem. –TBC

And ye shall not swear by my name falsely, neither shalt thou profane the name of thy God: I am the LORD.

—LEVITICUS 19:12

January 23

Why would God create anyone knowing that so many would go to hell? Imagine that before anyone was created, the uncreated souls of the 60 percent who would go to hell (I just picked a number) paraded before God's throne in a protest march demanding not to be created because of the fate that awaited them. But God says that they don't have to go to hell; He has made provision for them all to go to heaven. Moreover, it isn't possible not to create them, because the protestors would be the mothers and fathers, uncles, aunts, children, grandparents, etc., of the 40 percent who would go to heaven, and it would not be fair to deny them the eternal bliss of God's love just because the 60 percent were so stubborn that they would choose to consign themselves to hell. –TBC

Then shall he say also unto them on the left hand,
Depart from me, ye cursed, into everlasting fire,
prepared for the devil and his angels.

—MATTHEW 25:41

January 24

Christians did not give up the Sabbath: we were never under the Mosaic Law. We did not change the Sabbath from Saturday to Sunday. We worship on Sunday, the first day of the new week (Acts 20:7; 1 Corinthians 16:2), because that is the day Christ rose from the dead, bringing us into a new covenant relationship. The Sabbath pertained to the old creation: we belong to the new. It was for God's earthly people: our citizenship is in heaven. –TBC

And upon the first day of the week, when the disciples came together to break bread...

—Acts 20:7

January 25

Should a Christian participate in a movement to bring God back into the schools? Perhaps it might be wise to ask which "God" will be brought back. Not all of the groups contending for this "common goal" believe in the same God. —TBC

And what concord hath Christ with Belial? or what part hath he that believeth with an infidel? And what agreement hath the temple of God with idols?

—2 CORINTHIANS 6:15-16

January 26

In attempting to embrace and deny self at the same time, you end up with contradiction and fallacy. You try valiantly to rescue self-esteem/respect by saying that it must result from recognizing that God created us in His image. On the contrary, we have no more reason to esteem and respect ourselves because God created us than we have to esteem ourselves because God created the universe around us. We had no more to do with creating ourselves (including the new creation in Christ) than we had with creating the remainder of the universe, and thus have no basis from either for esteeming or respecting ourselves. –TBC

Humble yourselves therefore under the mighty hand of God, that he may exalt you in due time.

—1 PETER 5:6

January 27

Jesus was opposed by the religious leaders, whereas the common people heard him gladly. Likewise, the religious leaders of today also have their complex theological explanations to defend and their positions of preference and power to protect. They are the ones who are blinded by prejudice—simplicity of ideas and experience rarely blinds anyone, but leaves them all the more able to apprehend the truth. –TBC

But when the multitudes saw it, they marvelled,
and glorified God, which had given such power unto men.

—MATTHEW 9:8

January 28

Jesus didn't say that in order to be His disciples we must discover who we are in Christ, but that we must be done with who we are and begin to experience that it is no more I but Christ who lives in me; He must increase but I must decrease. Jesus said the requirement is to deny self. –TBC

I am crucified with Christ: nevertheless I live; yet not I, but Christ liveth in me: and the life which I now live in the flesh I live by the faith of the Son of God, who loved me, and gave himself for me.

—Galatians 2:20

January 29

Christianity needs no contribution from any source, and if it does, then the Bible has lied to us when it says that Christianity is Christ in you, the hope of glory. Nothing can be added to Galatians 2:20 and the transformation of life which that brings, or to 2 Corinthians 5:17–18, or to Galatians 5:22–23. The fruit of the Spirit (not of therapy!) is love, joy, peace, longsuffering, etc. Neither here nor anywhere else does the Bible give the impression that Christ has only a partial solution to offer or that Christianity needs help from some outside source! But Christian psychology is based upon this heretical premise; otherwise it would have no reason to exist! –TBC

Therefore if any man be in Christ, he is a new creature:
old things are passed away; behold, all things are become new.

—2 Corinthians 5:17

January 30

Consider the example of a potter who molds a perfect vase, decorates it with a beautiful glaze, and very carefully fires it so that at the end of the firing process it emerges from the kiln perfect in every aspect. He then places it on a shelf, where there is the possibility of it falling unless it is so securely bound that it becomes impossible to fall. In like manner, Adam and Eve were created perfect, but the Lord chose to not "bind" them in such a manner as to make it impossible for them to fall into sin. We do have free will. –TBC

But of the tree of the knowledge of good and evil, thou shalt not eat of it: for in the day that thou eatest thereof thou shalt surely die.

—Genesis 2:17

January 31

Remember that a false prophecy can also come to pass; the Bible tells us that in the last days all kinds of signs and wonders will take place, but they will not be of God! Have you not encountered people who are determined to believe whatever they believe, regardless? Hence the absolute importance of the Word of God, which is sharper than any two-edged sword. Only the Word can break rocks in pieces. Only the Word does what it sets out to do! –TBC

And the sign or the wonder come to pass, whereof he spake unto thee, saying, Let us go after other gods, which thou hast not known, and let us serve them…

—DEUTERONOMY 13:2

February

February 1

As we mature, the searchlight of the Holy Spirit's conviction causes us to see that we are nothing and can do nothing without Christ; that we are indeed empty vessels; that our joy originates from being flooded with the Holy Spirit's enablement in all things—and now we know that we are indeed abiding in the Vine, wonderfully and completely dependent and nourished. –TBC

I can do all things through Christ which strengtheneth me.

—Philippians 4:13

February 2

The power of God is not limited to working within a certain cultural or political setting, nor were the heroes and heroines of the faith in the Old and New Testaments limited by circumstances. Paul would let nothing stand in the way of his obeying God—so you may be certain that the lack of example of political or social activism in the Bible was not due to circumstances, setting, or anything other than the fact that it was not God's will. –TBC

The heavens declare the glory of God; and the firmament sheweth his handywork. Day unto day uttereth speech, and night unto night sheweth knowledge. There is no speech nor language, where their voice is not heard. Their line is gone out through all the earth, and their words to the end of the world.

—PSALM 19:1–4

February 3

Every faith teacher, from Wigglesworth to Bosworth, Copeland, or Price, or anyone else who has taught or teaches that no Christian need ever sicken or die, is himself either dead or dying. Thus, when we are praying for a sick person, we must commend them to God's will and care. Only if we receive a special revelation that it is God's will to heal this person at this time can we with assurance command the disease to depart in the Name of Jesus. –TBC

Erastus abode at Corinth: but
Trophimus have I left at Miletum sick.

—2 TIMOTHY 4:20

February 4

Playing around with what the Bible calls familiar spirits is a very dangerous practice. It was absolutely forbidden to our ancestors by God through Moses and the other prophets. This was not because God is mean or wanted to keep His people from something good, but because these spirits are not really who or what they claim to be, no matter what they call themselves, whether "spirits of the dead" or anything else. –TBC

And the man in whom the evil spirit was leaped on them, and overcame them, and prevailed against them, so that they fled out of that house naked and wounded.

—Acts 19:16

February 5

Every believer needs regular Christian fellowship and should be accountable to the leadership in some church. We won't find the perfect church, so we must be willing to settle for something less than that. We shouldn't try to impose our burden upon them but should go there for fellowship, prayer, and spiritual food. We can minister outside of that church until they accept us and ask us to minister there; we shouldn't force ourselves upon them. In the meantime, we must make certain that our personal walk with the Lord is pleasing to Him, that we are praising, loving, and worshiping Him, and that His joy is our strength. We are to be examples to others, not only in our concern for and opposition to the seduction in the church and the world but also in the victorious lives we live in Christ. —TBC

And let us consider one another to provoke unto love and to good works: Not forsaking the assembling of ourselves together, as the manner of some is; but exhorting one another: and so much the more, as ye see the day approaching.

—HEBREWS 10:24–25

February 6

The dog returns to his vomit because that's what dogs do. The sow returns to wallowing in the mire because that is what a hog does. Neither the dog nor the pig has had its nature changed. Neither has been "born again" or been changed into another species. The dog experienced a temporary purging and the sow underwent a washing. Neither "work" had any eternal meaning, no matter how it might have spruced up appearances—like the whitewashing of a tomb (Matthew 23:27). –TBC

But it is happened unto them according to the true proverb,
The dog is turned to his own vomit again; and the sow
that was washed to her wallowing in the mire.

—2 Peter 2:22

February 7

It is not true that the gifts of the Spirit passed away with the days of the apostles or the completion of the Scriptures, etc. That view simply cannot be sustained from the New Testament, as A. W. Tozer said so forcefully. Yet the "-isms" that have come to represent the belief in the gifts of the Spirit for today have been the nest of every foul bird and have promulgated much error; in fact there is far more error than truth in them today. —TBC

But the manifestation of the Spirit
is given to every man to profit withal.

—1 CORINTHIANS 12:7

February 8

To be tempted is not a sin (i.e., to be presented with a situation or circumstance that appeals to our innate appetites—James 1:12). Sin doesn't take place until the mind begins to dwell upon the temptation and yield to it (James 1:13–15). The Lord Jesus was tempted by everything that could possibly appeal to us, but He did not yield to the temptation. He did not allow His mind to dwell on impure things. He was "yet without sin" (Hebrews 4:15): "Who did no sin, neither was guile found in his mouth" (1 Peter 2:22). –TBC

But every man is tempted, when he is drawn away of his own lust, and enticed. Then when lust hath conceived, it bringeth forth sin: and sin, when it is finished, bringeth forth death.

—JAMES 1:14–15

February 9

When we rely on speculation to fill in areas not clearly addressed by Scripture, of necessity we create a situation generating even more questions. More questions are raised than satisfactory answers given when one begins to speculate. Sadly, some have been so taken up with speculative issues that their effectiveness for the kingdom is compromised. May God grant us the wisdom to know when and where to stand and what is necessary in order that we might "…therefore follow after the things which make for peace, and things wherewith one may edify another" (Romans 14:19). –TBC

He is proud, knowing nothing, but doting about questions and strifes of words, whereof cometh envy, strife, railings, evil surmisings.

—1 TIMOTHY 6:4

February 10

Experience of whatever kind absolutely cannot become our main focus, nor can we prove our interpretation of the Word by it. The Lord, however, certainly gives us, in His unique way, very precious confirmations and intimate assurances of His Word. The human tendency is to testify to these experiences, which then can lead to a number of problems. We must heed the Holy Spirit's direction. There are many examples of people in leadership who did not do so, which eventually led to pride, a superior attitude, imitating and covetousness by followers, and even entire ministries filled with error and imbalance. The works of God are indeed splendid and hand-tailored, but how we handle them must glorify Him and Him alone. –TBC

We have also a more sure word of prophecy; whereunto ye do well that ye take heed, as unto a light that shineth in a dark place, until the day dawn, and the day star arise in your hearts.

—2 PETER 1:19

February 11

Take comfort in the knowledge that our God is a God of mercy; that the depths of His grace are beyond our understanding; and that if even on this earth He is able to do exceedingly abundantly above and beyond that which we can ask or even think (Ephesians 3:20, 1 Corinthians 2:9), why can we not look forward with utmost confidence in Him regarding our every concern? This we know: when we see Him face to face, we will certainly agree with Him! —TBC

Blessed be God, even the Father of our Lord Jesus Christ, the Father of mercies, and the God of all comfort.

—2 Corinthians 1:3

February 12

When the Lord gave Paul his "Macedonian Call," the apostle didn't begin some form of prayer warfare against a supposed spiritual entity controlling Macedonia. He had such a relationship with the Lord that when his call came, he moved in obedience. Throughout this process, the Lord led Paul through many circumstances and situations (2 Corinthians 11:24–28). And throughout those circumstances, he had many faithful people praying for him (2 Corinthians 1:11). –TBC

And a vision appeared to Paul in the night; There stood a man of Macedonia, and prayed him, saying, Come over into Macedonia, and help us. And after he had seen the vision, immediately we endeavoured to go into Macedonia, assuredly gathering that the Lord had called us for to preach the gospel unto them.

—Acts 16:9–10

February 13

Jesus Himself gave the two disciples going to Emmaus a thorough lesson on the scriptural imperative: "Oh fools, and slow of heart to believe all that the prophets have spoken" (Luke 24:25). This reference to "the prophets" cannot be interpreted as "tradition and also the scriptures." Jesus is referring to the Scriptures alone: "And beginning at Moses and all the prophets, he expounded unto them in all the scriptures the things concerning himself" (Luke 24:27). If He held them accountable for their unbelief about the Scriptures, is it not a reasonable conclusion that they must have had access to the same? –TBC

Jesus answered and said unto them, Ye do err, not knowing the scriptures, nor the power of God.

—Matthew 22:29

February 14

We must avoid the mistake of many who are hung up on a concept or idea and who then seek to interpret the bulk of Scripture in a way that is supportive of that idea. –TBC

Even as our beloved brother Paul also according to the wisdom given unto him hath written unto you...some things hard to be understood, which they that are unlearned and unstable wrest, as they do also the other scriptures, unto their own destruction...beware lest ye also, being led away with the error of the wicked, fall from your own stedfastness.

—2 Peter 3:15–17

February 15

Although a Christian who seeks to walk in a holy and righteous manner will certainly enjoy better health as he avoids many things that can be injurious, nevertheless, we do live in a sin-cursed world where the rain falls on the just and unjust (Matthew 5:45), and where the second law of thermodynamics still holds sway. We all age, our body parts wear out, and some of us may be subject to physical problems much like the stomach problems that bothered Timothy (I Timothy 5:23). Many people were healed through the ministry of Paul, but to Timothy he gave some advice on how to relieve the symptoms of his physical problem. The same Apostle Paul also said, "and Trophimus have I left at Miletum sick" (2 Timothy 4:20). –TBC

Drink no longer water, but use a little wine for thy stomach's sake and thine often infirmities.

—1 TIMOTHY 5:23

February 16

God places into high office those whom He chooses, some of whom may be Christians. It is most telling that Joseph, Daniel, Hananiah, Azariah, Mishael, and others elevated by God into high governmental positions did not use the world's methods to achieve their positions. –TBC

There are certain Jews whom thou hast set over the affairs of the province of Babylon, Shadrach, Meshach, and Abednego; these men, O king, have not regarded thee: they serve not thy gods, nor worship the golden image which thou hast set up.

—DANIEL 3:12

February 17

Psychology is not a science. It involves hundreds of contradictory theories upon which psychologists can't even agree, and it has no place in a Christian college or seminary. –TBC

O Timothy, keep that which is committed to thy trust, avoiding profane and vain babblings, and oppositions of science falsely so called.

—1 Timothy 6:20

February 18

If you were drowning and someone offered to pull you from the water, and you accepted that offer, would it be true that you had done anything to save yourself? Could you say that you had been saved by your own works, and thereby become proud? What, then, of those who receive Christ by an act of their will—was it because they were smart enough, loving enough, wise enough, righteous enough, or anything else enough? That I choose to accept the pardon God offers in Christ does not constitute any work on my part. It is all of God and all by grace. I can take no credit whatsoever! —TBC

Not by works of righteousness which we have done, but according to his mercy he saved us, by the washing of regeneration, and renewing of the Holy Ghost.

—TITUS 3:5

February 19

The Bible declares that the clear indication of whether one who claims to be a prophet is in fact not a true prophet of God is if he contradicts what the Bible teaches (Isaiah 8:20). By that criterion, both Muhammad and Baha'u'llah (as well as Buddha, Krishna, et al.) are false prophets, because they clearly contradict the teachings of Jesus and His apostles, who built without contradiction upon the teachings of the Old Testament prophets. –TBC

To the law and to the testimony:
if they speak not according to this word,
it is because there is no light in them.

—Isaiah 8:20

February 20

We are told to earnestly contend for the faith, "to reprove, rebuke, exhort, and them that sin, rebuke before all" (2 Timothy 4:2; 1 Timothy 5:20). Surely there is no greater sin against God and His people than to lead astray with false doctrine! –TBC

Beloved, when I gave all diligence to write unto you of the common salvation, it was needful for me to write unto you, and exhort you that ye should earnestly contend for the faith which was once delivered unto the saints.

—JUDE 3

February 21

Man by his own understanding cannot discover God. We can only know Him as He reveals Himself—not as we imagine Him to be. And He has revealed Himself to the conscience, in His Word, and through His Son Jesus Christ. —TBC

And the Word was made flesh, and dwelt among us, (and we beheld his glory, the glory as of the only begotten of the Father,) full of grace and truth.

—John 1:14

February 22

To believe in some higher power is not enough. In fact, it could be the means of giving someone false hope and, in the end, damning them for eternity. —TBC

For though there be that are called gods, whether in heaven or in earth, (as there be gods many, and lords many,) But to us there is but one God, the Father, of whom are all things, and we in him; and one Lord Jesus Christ, by whom are all things, and we by him.

—1 CORINTHIANS 8:5–6

February 23

Although there are occasions when the Lord may permit individual Christians to participate as His instruments in the specific deliverance of an unsaved person from demons, no amount of ritual or ceremony will ever free anyone. Christ, and Christ alone, sets us free; He leaves the choice to us to seek and accept it. —TBC

If the Son therefore shall make you free, ye shall be free indeed.

—JOHN 8:36

February 24

To state that the Law was given specifically to Israel and not to the Gentiles is not to render a personal opinion, but simply to note what the Scriptures say. In Ezekiel 20:12, the Lord specifically states that He gave them (Israel) "my sabbaths, to be a sign between me and them, that they might know that I am the Lord that sanctify them." That this is a particular command to Israel is borne out by many other scriptures (Exodus 16:29; 31:14–16; Deuteronomy 5:15, etc.). Nothing like this is ever stated to the Gentiles. If it were otherwise, we should reasonably expect clear teaching in the New Testament stating so, particularly in Acts 15. Contrary to claims of overwhelming evidence, there is nothing to be found. –TBC

Wherefore the children of Israel shall keep the sabbath, to observe the sabbath throughout their generations, for a perpetual covenant.

—Exodus 31:16

February 25

Deliverance is something that every child of God receives as he is translated out of the kingdom of darkness and into the kingdom of light, and that he continues to receive as his life is transformed (Luke 11:4; 2 Corinthians 1:10; 2 Peter 2:9). The Bible emphasizes that He whom the Son sets free is free indeed. –TBC

The Lord knoweth how to deliver the godly out of temptations, and to reserve the unjust unto the day of judgment to be punished...

—2 Peter 2:9

February 26

The Bible is not the teacher of its own truth; that is the function of the Holy Spirit, who is given to every believer. And it is He who leads us into all truth, not some hierarchy in the church. —TBC

But the natural man receiveth not the things of the Spirit of God: for they are foolishness unto him: neither can he know them, because they are spiritually discerned.

—1 CORINTHIANS 2:14

February 27

It is a difficult and lifelong process for us to achieve submission and dependence. The greatest battle takes place in our mind. Romans 12:1–2 tells us to "present [our] bodies a living sacrifice. . . . And be not conformed to this world: but be ye transformed by the renewing of your mind." With this in mind, 2 Corinthians 10:4–5 tells us that "(the weapons of our warfare are not carnal [or fleshly], but mighty through God to the pulling down of strong holds;) casting down imaginations [or reasonings]...and bringing into captivity every thought to the obedience of Christ." The main battlefield is the human mind. –TBC

Thou hast put all things in subjection under his feet. For in that he put all in subjection under him, he left nothing that is not put under him. But now we see not yet all things put under him.

—Hebrews 2:8

February 28

Never do we get the idea from Scripture that Baal worship or the paganism of the heathen surrounding Israel had any good points. Nor is there any hint by Paul that the worship of Diana of the Ephesians or the paganism in Corinth had any good points in them but were to be totally rejected. –TBC

Thus saith the LORD, Learn not the way of the heathen, and be not dismayed at the signs of heaven, for the heathen are dismayed at them.

—JEREMIAH 10:2

February 29

It takes much love to be willing to correct. It would be far easier not to do so. Yet Jesus said, "As many as I love I rebuke and chasten." —TBC

As many as I love, I rebuke and chasten:
be zealous therefore, and repent.

—Revelation 3:19

March

March 1

Lack of formal training is in itself not a measure of one's calling. Consider the example of Peter and John, who astounded the religious teachers of their day: "Now when they saw the boldness of Peter and John, and perceived that they were unlearned and ignorant men, they marvelled; and they took knowledge of them, that they had been with Jesus" (Acts 4:13). Of greater concern than a lack of formal training would be a lack of sound teaching. –TBC

And when the sabbath day was come, he began to teach in the synagogue: and many hearing him were astonished, saying, From whence hath this man these things? and what wisdom is this which is given unto him, that even such mighty works are wrought by his hands?

—MARK 6:2

March 2

The Bible is filled with verses to the effect that the Good Shepherd will keep His sheep, that those to whom He gives eternal life shall never perish, that He who has begun a good work in us will perform it, and that even if all our works are burned up, yet the one who is in Christ is saved though as by fire. Never does the Bible say that the One who purchased my salvation has now turned it over to me to lose it if I please. That would be the utmost folly, and it is the force of the argument in Hebrews 6: that if one could be lost, it would be impossible to be saved without Christ being crucified again, in which case Christ would be made a fool of before the world for having procured salvation at such a cost and then turning it over to sinners who could never earn it and who surely can't keep it. —TBC

Now unto him that is able to keep you from falling, and to present you faultless before the presence of his glory with exceeding joy, To the only wise God our Saviour…

—JUDE 24–25

March 3

Regardless of what we might want the Scriptures to say, Paul very plainly says that he was "given…a thorn in the flesh" in order that he not fall into pride or be exalted above measure because of the abundance of the revelations. The loving God who created Paul knew every weakness of this man and what would be needed to keep him from falling prey to human pride. —TBC

And lest I should be exalted above measure through the abundance of the revelations, there was given to me a thorn in the flesh, the messenger of Satan to buffet me, lest I should be exalted above measure.

—2 Corinthians 12:7

March 4

No one even uses the terms "Christian chemistry" or "Christian aerodynamics," etc. Such terms would be meaningless, since these disciplines have nothing to do with Christianity. Then why use the term "Christian psychology"? Because it claims to deal with that which the Bible says is its sole province, and even to improve upon Christianity by supplying what is lacking in the Bible—and that is an abomination! Jesus said, I will send you another Comforter, the Spirit of truth, whom the world cannot receive (John 14:16–17); and when He, the Spirit of truth has come, He will lead you into all truth (John 16:13). Clearly, this truth that sets free does not involve science at all, since, if it did, then only Christians could make scientific discoveries. –TBC

...keep that which is committed to thy trust, avoiding profane and vain babblings, and oppositions of science falsely so called: Which some professing have erred concerning the faith.

—1 TIMOTHY 6:20–21

March 5

God did not get a bargain; He didn't pay equal value—what I am worth. The great cost at which I was redeemed gives me no cause to have a sense of self-worth but of shame that the consequences of my sin caused Christ to pay such a great price. The shedding of Christ's blood, with which we were redeemed, was not because of our worth but because of our sin and the demands of God's justice. So, the greater the price, the worse the sin. To associate this purchase price with the value of an object to God, and to make it the basis for self-worth, is neither biblical nor logical. In fact, it shows the perversion that is caused by the influence of selfist psychology. –TBC

For ye are bought with a price: therefore glorify God in your body, and in your spirit, which are God's.

—1 Corinthians 6:20

March 6

Man is morally responsible to say yes to God's offer of mercy, and he is a fool who does not do so. We cannot love either God or one another without the capacity to choose to do so. Love must come from the heart. –TBC

Beloved, let us love one another: for love is of God; and every one that loveth is born of God, and knoweth God.

—1 JOHN 4:7

March 7

Many people challenge God to rise up and demonstrate His love in a tangible way. God says to us, however, "Awake thou that sleepest, and arise from the dead, and Christ shall give thee light" (Ephesians 5:14). What more tangible proof of God should we require than what Christ has already done on the Cross? Have you appropriated it? "Him that cometh to me I will in no wise cast out" (John 6:37). Others say that "Jesus Christ seems ethereal, nebulous, far away, and removed from my everyday struggles," and God seems "very impersonal." In contrast, the Scriptures tell us that when we draw nigh to God, He will draw nigh to us. Was this a lie? –TBC

That they should seek the Lord, if haply they might feel after him, and find him, though he be not far from everyone of us…

—Acts 17:27

March 8

When we continue to desire and seek all that the Lord is, and to please Him rather than to get something from Him, letting the Holy Spirit be our teacher, as Scripture promises, and letting Him lead us into all truth through the Scriptures (and not through experiential teachings), we will find Him richly blessing us with all that He has for us (Matthew 6:33). —TBC

Thus saith the LORD, thy Redeemer, the Holy One of Israel; I am the LORD thy God which teacheth thee to profit, which leadeth thee by the way that thou shouldest go.

—ISAIAH 48:17

March 9

Be assured that the moment you placed your trust in Jesus Christ for your salvation and accepted Him as your Savior, the Holy Spirit, now dwelling within you, began the process of enabling you to lead a holy life (John 14:16). Therefore you need not question or doubt your salvation because of any doubt about having received the Holy Spirit. –TBC

And if Christ be in you, the body is dead because of sin;
but the Spirit is life because of righteousness.

—Romans 8:10

March 10

The Roman Catholic system is in a difficult position regarding the Bible. On the one hand, they profess to hold it in esteem, and yet, on the other hand, it can be demonstrated that many of their traditions do not originate within the pages of Scripture. —TBC

Thus have ye made the commandment of God
of none effect by your tradition.

—MATTHEW 15:6

March 11

Christ's claims, if taken at face value, condemn as false all other religions. He claims to be the way, the truth, the life, and that no one can come to God except through Him. It is fundamentally dishonest to treat His claims as though they are in harmony with all other religions, when, in fact, that is not the case. You cannot embrace Christianity and any other religion at the same time. If what Christ said is true, then all other religions are false and their leaders frauds. —TBC

Because ye have said, We have made a covenant with death,
and with hell are we at agreement; when the overflowing scourge
shall pass through, it shall not come unto us: for we have made
lies our refuge, and under falsehood have we hid ourselves.

—Isaiah 28:15

March 12

We often put a selfish interpretation on the Scripture that says of Jesus, "For the joy that was set before him, he endured the cross, despising the shame...." We think it was the pleasure of having us in His presence, and certainly, that played a large part. However, it is apparent from the Word of God that the real joy set before Him was knowing that He had fulfilled His Father's will—that He had been true to His commitment, to His purpose at coming into this world, and that He had pleased His Father. —TBC

I have glorified thee on the earth: I have finished the work which thou gavest me to do.

—JOHN 17:4

March 13

Concerning the charge that Christians should be observing the feasts and holidays given specifically to the Jews in the Old Testament, the Scriptures clearly teach that Christ came to fulfill the law (Matthew 5:17) and the church is no longer under the law (Romans 6:14). Further, Galatians was written to those who denied this teaching, pointing out that the Law was our schoolmaster to bring us to Christ and therefore no longer necessary. Finally, decisions rendered by the early church leadership in Acts 15–16 say nothing about observing the festivals and other practices given to the nation of Israel (Exodus 19:3–6). –TBC

Wherefore the law was our schoolmaster to bring us unto Christ, that we might be justified by faith.

—Galatians 3:24

March 14

It is only because Christ is God come down as a Man, without sin of His own and thus able to die for the sins of others, that He could pay the debt demanded by infinite justice. And it is on that righteous basis of the debt having been paid in full that He now offers full pardon and eternal life with Him in heaven. —TBC

And without controversy great is the mystery of godliness: God was manifest in the flesh, justified in the Spirit, seen of angels, preached unto the Gentiles, believed on in the world, received up into glory .

—1 TIMOTHY 3:16

March 15

It is one thing to recognize that some Catholics are truly saved in spite of the system, but another thing entirely to accept the unity promoted today, which lends legitimacy to the system itself. We love Catholics, just as we love all mankind, and want them to know Christ, but to be saved, they must believe the gospel—not what Rome teaches. Furthermore, Catholicism itself has made it very clear that it will never change. The more than 100 anathemas that have been pronounced against biblical Christianity are found in the Canons and Decrees of the Council of Trent. Therefore, any unity with Rome would involve an abandonment of the "faith which was once delivered unto the saints" (Jude 3). May God deliver us from such concession. —TBC

Can two walk together, except they be agreed?

—AMOS 3:3

March 16

It is not enough to call a person to Jesus as the best means of getting rid of their addiction. There is the matter of sin. The fact that He died for our sins upon the Cross, was buried, and rose again the third day, is the gospel by which we are saved, and to leave that out is to preach a false Jesus and a false gospel. –TBC

For I delivered unto you first of all that which I also received, how that Christ died for our sins according to the scriptures; And that he was buried, and that he rose again the third day according to the scriptures.

—1 Corinthians 15:3–4

March 17

A mark of a true Christian is that he or she continues to be convicted of past and present sins as the Holy Spirit continues working. Rejoice, because that shows you're growing! Indeed, our maturing in the Lord will continue as long as we live until we're glorified in His presence. That which He began in you He will perfect at that day! –TBC

Being confident of this very thing, that he which hath begun a good work in you will perform it until the day of Jesus Christ.

—PHILIPPIANS 1:6

March 18

Although it is true that some have a more intimate relationship with God due to diligent practice, this status is not reserved to a select few. Paul desired that "ye might be filled with the knowledge of his will in all wisdom and spiritual understanding" (Colossians 1:9). Peter ended his second epistle with the admonition to "grow in grace, and in the knowledge of our Lord and Saviour Jesus Christ. To him be glory both now and for ever. Amen" (2 Peter 3:18). May God encourage us to that end. —TBC

And Enoch walked with God: and he was not; for God took him.

—Genesis 5:24

March 19

Frustration for Christians often comes from our own lack of progress—our failure to purge our lives of influences such as books, magazines, television programs, acquaintances, that create footholds for the adversary to manipulate or that simply indicate a lack of discipline in key areas of our lives. –TBC

But have renounced the hidden things of dishonesty, not walking in craftiness, nor handling the word of God deceitfully; but by manifestation of the truth commending ourselves to every man's conscience in the sight of God.

—2 CORINTHIANS 4:2

March 20

We should be as wise as we can, and certainly we should be loving and kind. But that is not the key to winning others. If it were, Jesus Christ would have won the world of His day and would not even have been crucified. No one was more patient and loving and kind and understanding than He. Yet they hated Him without a cause and crucified Him. He says very clearly that the servant is not greater than his Lord and that the world will hate us just as it hated Him. The only thing that will win people to Christ is God's truth. They must become lovers of Truth. They must have a passion for Truth. If not, all of our love and patience and building bridges in whatever ways we conceive will not win them to Christ. –TBC

Behold, I send you forth as sheep in the midst of wolves: be ye therefore wise as serpents, and harmless as doves.

—Matthew 10:16

March 21

Consider Psalm 119, which is written from the aspect of someone who is attempting to grow in his relationship with the Lord. Verse 9 asks, "[How] shall a young man cleanse his way?" It answers, "By taking heed thereto according to thy word." The disciples asked Jesus what they must do to work the works of God. He answered, "This is the work of God, that ye believe on him whom he hath sent" (John 6:28–29). In other words, our task is simply to believe, to take our first baby steps, and to let God take care of the rest. —TBC

Believe on the Lord Jesus Christ, and thou shalt be saved.

—ACTS 16:31

March 22

There is no greater joy for any of us, in the final analysis, than knowing that we have done God's will, that we have pleased Him, that we have been true to His Word, to His love, and that we have responded in kind to His grace and commitment to us. If we keep these things in mind, it helps to stabilize our Christian life, gives us a real purpose and joy in simply being and saying and doing what He has planned for us. And that is a joy that will be ours for all eternity. Anything that violates this brings us temporary pleasure but lasting remorse. —TBC

I have fought a good fight, I have finished my course, I have kept the faith.

—2 TIMOTHY 4:7

March 23

As we grow and mature in the Lord, we become more Christlike. We "reflect" His attitudes and we show His working in our lives. As the lesser light of the moon is just a reflection of the greater light of the sun, so we only reflect the image of the Son. Therefore, to become more Christlike is simply to conform our lives, our attitudes, and our minds to Him. –TBC

And be not conformed to this world: but be ye transformed by the renewing of your mind, that ye may prove what is that good, and acceptable, and perfect, will of God.

—ROMANS 12:2

March 24

Despite the accusations of those who deny the security of the believer, it is not true that those who believe it try to see how much they can get by with. The writer of Hebrews warns that the Lord chastens His disobedient children (Hebrews 12:1–11). Let us be as those of whom this same writer spoke, of whom he was persuaded better things, "things that accompany salvation" (Hebrews 6:9). —TBC

And ye have forgotten the exhortation which speaketh unto you as unto children, My son, despise not thou the chastening of the Lord, nor faint when thou art rebuked of him: For whom the Lord loveth he chasteneth, and scourgeth every son whom he receiveth.

—HEBREWS 12:5–6

March 25

You know the tragic result of well-meaning pastors and faith healers who continue to command diseases to depart and nothing happens. This goes on thousands of times a day around the world. What do you think that does to the faith of a young person growing up in such circles? No wonder they think Christianity doesn't work—and despise the hypocrisy of those who claim that it does, obvious appearances to the contrary. –TBC

But there were false prophets also among the people,
even as there shall be false teachers among you,
who privily shall bring in damnable heresies . . .
And many shall follow their pernicious ways;
by reason of whom the way of truth
shall be evil spoken of.

—2 PETER 2:1-2

March 26

Why so few miracles today? Because the emphasis is upon healing instead of holiness, upon the gifts instead of the Giver—and because those who profess these gifts have largely rejected the clear teaching of Scripture concerning them. We do not intend to deny the validity of the gifts for today. But most of what goes on out there in the name of the gifts of the Spirit is not of God. The problem today is that much of what is being passed off as the work of the Holy Spirit is fleshly at best and demonic at worst. –TBC

And those members of the body, which we think to be less honourable, upon these we bestow more abundant honour; and our uncomely parts have more abundant comeliness. For our comely parts have no need: but God hath tempered the body together, having given more abundant honour to that part which lacked.

—1 Corinthians 12:23–24

March 27

"Praying always" speaks of our attitude toward the Lord—not the frequency or duration of our praying. Prayer is simply communication with our Creator. As one missionary pointed out, there is much praying going on, but precious little prayer. We see an example in Scripture of Nehemiah, a man who was in constant communication with God. When standing before the king of Persia, Nehemiah was asked what he desired. His immediate response was "I prayed to the God of heaven." Clearly, he did not get down on his knees and pray aloud in the presence of the king, but his attitude of constant prayer enabled him to call out to God in his mind. It was the natural thing to do. –TBC

Pray without ceasing.

—1 THESSALONIANS 5:17

March 28

The Scriptures clearly teach that if one does not have the Holy Spirit, one is not saved and therefore, one is not a Christian. There is no intermediate state of belief. To state otherwise is once again to add words that obscure both plain meaning and context. As Acts is a historical account (and not a doctrinal book) of what happened to specific people at specific times for our admonition, we must look to the epistles for the explanation of why and how and what happened. Too many groups have tried to stamp out cookie-cutter Christians by exalting Acts above the witness of the rest of Scripture. In this, they forget that God doesn't stamp out uniform bricks, but He is building His church with living stones. To make one's experience the determinant of interpretation is a doorway to error. Too many people confront the plain teaching of Scripture and dismiss it with, "So what? I've got a testimony." —TBC

But ye are not in the flesh, but in the Spirit, if so be that the Spirit of God dwell in you. Now if any man have not the Spirit of Christ, he is none of his.

—ROMANS 8:9

March 29

The bottom line is to know the Scriptures thoroughly, to remain open to the leading of the Holy Spirit, and to intercede as you await the opportunities the Lord can give you—remembering, too, that the church without spot or wrinkle for whom the Lord Jesus Christ will return is not going to be an institutional one but made up of those who are truly His. Putting it another way, we will continue to see apostasy and delusion, the Scriptures tell us. We must remain faithful, diligent, watchful, and not grow discouraged at what we may see in the churches about us. –TBC

And let us not be weary in well doing: for in due season we shall reap, if we faint not.

—GALATIANS 6:9

March 30

Pragmatism in church growth (including being geared to psychological counseling, felt needs, entertainment, etc.) can lead to problems. One of the inherent risks is that a pastor or leader could be distracted from the prime focus of God's own leading for him in his particular situation and mesmerized by another man's success into an all-out implementation of someone else's program. As always, it remains for any Christian to maintain discernment and a Berean perspective in the face of strong programs or example, inspired by what God is doing in someone's life or ministry but not easily swept into its vortex. –TBC

Beware lest any man spoil you through philosophy and vain deceit, after the tradition of men, after the rudiments of the world, and not after Christ.

—Colossians 2:8

March 31

The devil presents counterfeits of all of God's blessings to pull us away from faith in God, and, as a result, it shouldn't be surprising that demonic signs and wonders exist—or that there are people who get some information from demonic sources. The whole world (the unsaved) lies under the sway of the wicked one (Satan). The unsaved are his, and although they're ultimately responsible for their actions, he has varying degrees of control in their lives. Only Christ can set one free from the bondage of sin and Satan. Without Christ, the only protection an unbeliever has is his or her own will, which is rarely a match for the schemes of the devil. —TBC

For such are false apostles, deceitful workers, transforming themselves into the apostles of Christ. And no marvel; for Satan himself is transformed into an angel of light.

—2 Corinthians 11:13–14

April

April 1

No human life (the body) is infinite (Hebrews 9:27). Part of the nature of the Lord Jesus Christ included a physical body that physically died on the Cross. The infinite part of Christ (His spirit) suffered the infinite pain of separation as He hung on the Cross for all mankind (Matthew 27:46). The most horrid part of the ordeal involved the time of separation from His father, with whom He was one (John 10:30). This oneness is something that our finite minds cannot comprehend. Neither can we comprehend the infinity involved. Furthermore, after His resurrection, the Lord Jesus continued to bear in His body the marks of His triumph—something He will do for eternity (John 20:24–29). –TBC

And as it is appointed unto men once to die,
but after this the judgment…

—HEBREWS 9:27

April 2

Where did Jesus go from the Cross? Jesus was able to say to the thief on the cross, "This day you will be with me in paradise," because "this day" was when He died; His body went into the tomb, but His spirit and soul were in paradise. –TBC

And Jesus said unto him, Verily I say unto thee,
To day shalt thou be with me in paradise.

—Luke 23:43

April 3

It is significant that the Greek word for "taste" in Hebrews 6 is the same word used of Jesus when He tasted death. The Greek word translated "taste" implies a brief acquaintance with, or something that is temporary. This would certainly agree with the Lord's experience. Death had no dominion over Christ. It was only temporary. So was the experience of those in Hebrews 6:4–6. They were tasters; they never fully ingested Christ in their lives. —TBC

For it is impossible for those who were once enlightened, and have tasted of the heavenly gift, and were made partakers of the Holy Ghost, And have tasted the good word of God, and the powers of the world to come, If they shall fall away, to renew them again unto repentance.

—HEBREWS 6:4–6

April 4

As for the blood of Christ that saves and cleanses, His blood would not save if He had merely bled a pint or two or given transfusions to mankind—it had to be all poured out in death. And just as there is no blood left from the unresurrected flesh coursing through His resurrected body, so there is none preserved in heaven, as though it had magical qualities. –TBC

For where a testament is, there must also of necessity be the death of the testator. For a testament is of force after men are dead: otherwise it is of no strength at all while the testator liveth.

—HEBREWS 9:16–17

April 5

There is no contradiction between Jesus' dying for the whole world and John's apparent assertion that He came only for those whom the Father had given him. John 3:16 very eloquently states that the Father gave His Son for the entire world that "whosoever believeth should not perish." Sadly, however, even though everyone would have the opportunity, not everyone would take advantage of the same. As John stated earlier, "He came unto his own, and his own received him not. But as many as received him, to them gave he power to become the sons of God, even to them that believe on his name" (John 1:11–12). –TBC

For God so loved the world, that he gave his only begotten Son, that whosoever believeth in him should not perish, but have everlasting life.

—John 3:16

April 6

Some Muslims have challenged the Lord Jesus Christ's dying for all mankind. As proof they offer Deuteronomy 24:16, which states, "The fathers shall not be put to death for the children, neither shall the children be put to death for the fathers: every man shall be put to death for his own sin." Although the verse repeats the theme that we all must pay for our sins, if we consider the implications, it also highlights how great the sacrifice of the Lord Jesus Christ was. –TBC

I am crucified with Christ: nevertheless I live; yet not I, but Christ liveth in me: and the life which I now live in the flesh I live by the faith of the Son of God, who loved me, and gave himself for me.

—Galatians 2:20

April 7

If the one sacrifice Christ made of Himself for sin was not enough to pay the full debt owed to God's justice—and take us to heaven—then what is? The Bible tells us clearly and repeatedly that Christ's death, burial, and resurrection were obtained for those who believe eternal salvation. –TBC

But this man, after he had offered one sacrifice for sins for ever, sat down on the right hand of God.

—Hebrews 10:12

April 8

Is it the Holy Spirit or the Father who draws us? It is possible that any disagreement lies in semantics. God is a Spirit, declares the scripture (John 4:24) and He is also holy (Psalm 22:3). Therefore, we might be splitting hairs to argue that the Father draws us and the Holy Spirit never does. Indeed, as fallible humans, we would have great difficulty in trying to fully compartmentalize the functions of the Godhead! –TBC

And I, if I be lifted up from the earth,
will draw all men unto me.

—JOHN 12:32

April 9

Instead of trusting in the Church and its sacraments, why not believe in the Lord Jesus Christ and receive eternal life as a free gift of His grace? He will take you to heaven if you die, and if you are still alive when He returns, He will take you to heaven without dying, if you only trust Him. –TBC

For by grace are ye saved through faith;
and that not of yourselves: it is the gift of God:
Not of works, lest any man should boast.

—Ephesians 2:8–9

April 10

The Lord knew very well the heart of man, and He consequently built safeguards into His Word in order to have a standard by which we might judge everything, as He commands. And we are specifically commanded to judge (I Thessalonians 5:21). First Corinthians 14 was given that we might have a way to determine the false from the true. –TBC

Judge not according to the appearance,
but judge righteous judgment.

—John 7:24

April 11

One may plant, another may water, but it is God who gives the increase. Rest in the faithfulness of our God and trust Him to give you exactly what you should say to each person. How thankful we can be that it is the Holy Spirit who convicts and leads into all truth. –TBC

Let your speech be alway with grace,
seasoned with salt, that ye may know
how ye ought to answer every man.

—COLOSSIANS 4:6

April 12

If you want to know the will of the Lord, walk in the way the Lord wants you to walk and do the things that are both pleasing to Him as well as most edifying to you—learn more about the Lord. The Scriptures are your door to this knowledge. By continued immersion in His Word, we learn about Him and learn to follow Him. –TBC

Trust in the LORD with all thine heart; and lean not unto thine own understanding. In all thy ways acknowledge him, and he shall direct thy paths.

—PROVERBS 3:5–6

April 13

It's important to realize that those in the Muslim world (and elsewhere) view everyone from the U.S. as being Christian. Unfortunately, their view of "Christians" is not helped along by the immorality and excesses they see about the people in America on television. —TBC

Not every one that saith unto me, Lord, Lord, shall enter into the kingdom of heaven; but he that doeth the will of my Father which is in heaven.

—MATTHEW 7:21

April 14

If we've become faithful servants, keeping our eyes fixed not upon death but upon Jesus, the author and finisher of our faith (Hebrews 12:2), we will be less likely to succumb to the one sorrow at death: no, not even the farewell to loved ones, but the regret that while on earth we could have done more in the Kingdom. —TBC

Wherefore seeing we also are compassed about with so great a cloud of witnesses, let us lay aside every weight, and the sin which doth so easily beset us, and let us run with patience the race that is set before us, Looking unto Jesus the author and finisher of our faith; who for the joy that was set before him endured the cross, despising the shame, and is set down at the right hand of the throne of God.

—Hebrews 12:1–2

April 15

The Lord would like to do an amazing work through each of us. But we are all different. That difference is absolutely crucial in serving the Lord and requires that we seek Him first (Matthew 6:33), keep our eyes fixed on Him (Hebrews 12:2), and become His workmanship (Ephesians 2:10). In all these things we can rejoice that Christ is "made unto us wisdom...that he that glorieth, let him glory in the Lord" (1 Corinthians 1:30–31). –TBC

But of him are ye in Christ Jesus, who of God is made unto us wisdom, and righteousness, and sanctification, and redemption.

—1 Corinthians 1:30

April 16

We are not told that Joseph or David, for example, needed deep emotional healing in the areas of identity and rejection. They found their comfort and joy in the Lord, forgot themselves, and became God's channels of blessing to others. And to those who say that this is too harsh for the average Christian to live up to, it is what the Lord requires, and we have His promise that He will bear our burdens and give us His comfort and strength. The Scripture does not say, "Rejoice in the LORD, unless you are too depressed or have been rejected and need deep emotional healing to deal with it"! It says, "Rejoice in the LORD always…and the joy of the LORD is your strength"! –TBC

And David was greatly distressed; for the people spake of stoning him, because the soul of all the people was grieved, every man for his sons and for his daughters: but David encouraged himself in the LORD his God.

—1 SAMUEL 30:6

April 17

Sin leaves marks on us. Consider the alcoholic, who, after years of heavy drinking, gives his life to the Lord. Do all the wrinkles and marks of a hard life suddenly smooth out? Of course not. Paul tells us that we are to live our Christian lives by "forgetting those things which are behind, and reaching forth unto those things which are before" (Philippians 3:13). How can we expect to make any progress if we are continually spending all our time agonizing over the things of the past? May God lift our hearts and our eyes that we might learn to look less at ourselves and more at Him (2 Corinthians 3:18). –TBC

Be not deceived; God is not mocked: for whatsoever
a man soweth, that shall he also reap.

—Galatians 6:7

April 18

Christ said that He will say to false prophets, "I never knew you!" There is no hint that any of those to whom He refers in Matthew 7:21–23 had once been saved and then lost their salvation, which surely must be the case if the "falling away" doctrine is correct. Why didn't the Lord say that they'd fallen from grace, rather than that they'd never been His—or at least include some people in that category? In fact, He makes no such statement. —TBC

Many will say to me in that day, Lord, Lord, have we not prophesied in thy name? and in thy name have cast out devils? and in thy name done many wonderful works? And then will I profess unto them, I never knew you: depart from me, ye that work iniquity.

—Matthew 7:22–23

April 19

Material blessing is no indication of God's acceptance. Many cults are indeed wealthy beyond the dreams of most Americans, but wealth is, in and of itself, no sign of God's blessing. On the contrary, David wrote that he had "seen the wicked in great power, and spreading himself like a green bay tree" (Psalm 37:35). —TBC

Charge them that are rich in this world, that they be not highminded, nor trust in uncertain riches, but in the living God, who giveth us richly all things to enjoy.

—1 TIMOTHY 6:17

April 20

We don't always see how much of an impact we've had on someone. But we're to witness in faith, and the Lord will often open unprecedented, unimagined further opportunities—and give wisdom abundantly to meet those opportunities. However, a faithful intercessor who has laid much groundwork, though he may look forward to being mightily used in a more active way, must also be prepared to rejoice without rancor should the Lord choose someone else to participate in the culmination of the intercessor's labors. Having prayed diligently and witnessed in faith, we can leave it with the Lord and trust Him. –TBC

I have planted, Apollos watered; but God gave the increase.
So then neither is he that planteth any thing, neither he
that watereth; but God that giveth the increase.

—1 CORINTHIANS 3:6–7

April 21

Trusting Jesus for salvation involves turning from one's sin. It is irrational to imagine that Christ took the penalty so that we could continue in sin. The promise that whosoever believes in Christ shall not perish (John 3:16) implies that if we do not repent by turning to Christ through believing in Him, we shall surely perish. –TBC

I tell you, Nay: but, except ye repent, ye shall all likewise perish.

—Luke 13:5

April 22

The Lord Jesus very emphatically stated that the one who looks on a woman to lust after her has committed adultery with her already in his heart. The issue here, of course, is that the battle against sin is won or lost in the mind (James 1:13–14). Consider the many Scriptures warning against setting anything vain or profane before our eyes. There are too many things in this evil age that conspire against the integrity of our marriages. We don't need to increase the odds against the success of the most important relationship (aside from with the Lord) that we have. "Let us lay aside every weight, and the sin which doth so easily beset us, and let us run with patience the race that is set before us" (Hebrews 12:1). –TBC

But I say unto you, That whosoever looketh on a woman to lust after her hath committed adultery with her already in his heart.

—MATTHEW 5:28

April 23

Lack of doctrinal concern in favor of the experiential is a danger. Although the Lord can work any way He wants to, man tries to institutionalize, formulate, and train to do something that only the Holy Spirit may do. –TBC

As also in all his epistles, speaking in them of these things; in which are some things hard to be understood, which they that are unlearned and unstable wrest, as they do also the other scriptures, unto their own destruction.

—2 Peter 3:16

April 24

Ephesians, chapter 5, provides examples on how Christians are to treat each other. It begins with an admonition to walk in love. This includes the husband and wife relationship, which it addresses in verses 20–33. These are not verses to use as sledgehammers on each other but rather things we each need to read, comprehend, and obey. Otherwise, we must certainly answer a question the Lord Jesus Christ asked, "And why call ye me, Lord, Lord, and do not the things which I say?" (Luke 6:46). –TBC

Be ye therefore followers of God, as dear children; And walk in love, as Christ also hath loved us, and hath given himself for us an offering and a sacrifice to God for a sweetsmelling savor.

—EPHESIANS 5:1–2

April 25

Remember that there is no condemnation in Christ Jesus. And consider this: If you feel that you have to forgive yourself, you are in danger of assuming the prerogatives of God. You say that the accuser is still trying to rob you of peace and joy. That's not something he'll stop trying to do, so you might as well get used to his attempts, refuse to allow them, and rejoice that you qualify as a target! Set your face like a flint and stop focusing on yourself (Romans 12:3), on the past (Hebrews 12:1,2), or on the darts of the enemy (Ephesians 6:16). Focus on Christ, on what He's done, on what He offers you, and on what you're doing to Him when you won't receive it. –TBC

There is therefore now no condemnation to them which are in Christ Jesus, who walk not after the flesh, but after the Spirit.

—Romans 8:1

April 26

Because Paul came to understand suffering, he gave testimony that he had come to the place where he could "take pleasure in infirmities, in reproaches, in necessities, in persecutions, in distresses..." (2 Corinthians 12:10). Was Paul a masochist who took pleasure in discomforts? Never! He understood that the deceitful heart of man (Romans 7:14–25) needed something to keep it under control; he very clearly said, "...for when I am weak, then am I strong" (2 Corinthians 12:10). –TBC

My brethren, count it all joy when ye fall into divers temptations; knowing this, that the trying of your faith worketh patience.

—James 1:2–3

April 27

Haven't you seen many choruses written at "milk" level? Most congregations, however, contain a mix of ages and include individuals whose spiritual maturity and growth causes a longing for "meat." In a service, should we not expect a glorious mixture of simple and complex—of milk and meat that minister to all generations? —TBC

Let the word of Christ dwell in you richly in all wisdom; teaching and admonishing one another in psalms and hymns and spiritual songs, singing with grace in your hearts to the Lord.

—COLOSSIANS 3:16

April 28

Questions are very good things, but we don't get all the answers at once. David said he loved to go about (some versions say "inquire about") the altar of the Lord—loving Him and seeking to know Him more and more deeply. This is the only real basis for asking our spiritual questions. –TBC

One thing have I desired of the LORD, that will I seek after; that I may dwell in the house of the LORD all the days of my life, to behold the beauty of the LORD, and to enquire in his temple.

—PSALM 27:4

April 29

While the Scriptures assure us that "My sheep will know My voice," they do not teach us in six easy lessons how to know His voice. Such teaching is best left to the Holy Spirit, who is perfectly capable. The bottom line is that we need to be Bereans, testing everything by the Scriptures. Ultimately, each of us is accountable to the Lord for our position and beliefs, and the "I had bad teaching" defense can't be expected to excuse us. –TBC

And ye said, Behold, the LORD our God hath shewed us his glory and his greatness, and we have heard his voice out of the midst of the fire: we have seen this day that God doth talk with man, and he liveth.

—DEUTERONOMY 5:24

April 30

Why is God letting His own people, who are asking for revival and fasting and praying, find a counterfeit? It is good to remember what Paul told us about these times: "For the time will come when they will not endure sound doctrine; but after their own lusts shall they heap to themselves teachers, having itching ears…" (2 Timothy 4:3). According to this verse, the only real seeking going on here is for self-gratification. –TBC

For there shall arise false Christs, and false prophets,
and shall shew great signs and wonders; insomuch that,
if it were possible, they shall deceive the very elect.

—Matthew 24:24

May

May 1

The strength and protection of the Lord, working in and through married believers in harmony, is invincible. It is His will, and it is much to be desired and sought. –TBC

Husbands, love your wives, even as Christ also loved the church, and gave himself for it.

—Ephesians 5:25

May 2

In this age, the emphasis is often on a nonoffensive, nonconfrontational gospel; but such a gospel is disobedient to the command of Christ (Matthew 28:19–20). There is only one gospel. It is eternal and changeless. It is the gospel of the Kingdom—the only gospel that Jesus or His disciples or Paul preached, and the same gospel that we must preach today. Unfortunately, seldom is the gospel preached in the way Paul preached it in Romans 1, Acts 17:2–3, etc. Chapter 1 of Romans, for example, reveals what must shock a Jew: that Christianity is not some new invention but the fulfillment of the same message that the Hebrew prophets had proclaimed. –TBC

And this gospel of the kingdom shall be preached in all the world for a witness unto all nations; and then shall the end come.

—MATTHEW 24:14

May 3

Concerning the Christian woman and church leadership, let the Bible speak for itself through I Corinthians 11:3; I Corinthians 14:33–35,40, and Titus 2:3–5. The plain language of Scripture would seem to preclude a woman's leadership role as pastor or teacher over men in a church context (I Timothy 2:12). Scripture would seemingly make allowance, however, for a woman's role in prayer or prophecy (I Corinthians 11:5) and in teaching other women (Titus 2:4). –TBC

But I suffer not a woman to teach, nor to usurp authority over the man, but to be in silence.

—1 TIMOTHY 2:12

May 4

Many of the social, family, economic, and spiritual problems that exist today may be traced to the failure of women to properly understand and carry out their scriptural roles. Sadly, even many Christian women, deceived by the temporal and often illusory status that they may gain in the world, have forfeited fulfillment of their special and pivotal place in God's plan. It's so easy to exchange the truth for a lie. –TBC

And the LORD God said, It is not good that the man should be alone; I will make him an help meet for him.

—GENESIS 2:18

May 5

Many individuals, whether religious or not, are capable of meritorious works. As Paul wrote in I Corinthians 13, "…and though I bestow all my goods to feed the poor, and though I give my body to be burned, and have not love, it profits me nothing." In other words, if we do many acts of kindness and yet do not share the true gospel with individuals, we have not helped them in the area where the most help is needed. –TBC

But we are all as an unclean thing, and all our righteousnesses are as filthy rags; and we all do fade as a leaf; and our iniquities, like the wind, have taken us away.

—Isaiah 64:6

May 6

Christ's death made possible and available the forgiveness of the sins of everyone in the world, but this forgiveness is effective only to whosoever believeth (John 5:24; 6:40; 11:25–26). When saved persons ask for the forgiveness of a sin today that was forgiven centuries ago on the Cross, they are essentially recognizing the availability of forgiveness and accepting that forgiveness as I John 1:9 tells them to do. Asking the Lord for forgiveness is a natural outflowing of confession—evidence of our confidence that indeed it is available and received. –TBC

Verily, verily, I say unto you, He that heareth my word, and believeth on him that sent me, hath everlasting life, and shall not come into condemnation; but is passed from death unto life.

—John 5:24

May 7

Jesus told us to go into all the world—not to be of it but certainly to go into it—and the world is everywhere, including in the churches. For this reason, although we dare not be presumptuous or arrogant, at the same time we need not be fearful or reluctant to go anywhere if we have asked the Lord where, when, and how He wants us to go. In fact, He can provide wonderful opportunities in unique situations. –TBC

But ye shall receive power, after that the Holy Ghost is come upon you: and ye shall be witnesses unto me both in Jerusalem, and in all Judaea, and in Samaria, and unto the uttermost part of the earth.

—Acts 1:8

May 8

What Islam does to those who grow up in it is horrible, yet how many of us have a burden for this largest group of lost souls on our planet? –TBC

And others save with fear, pulling them out of the fire; hating even the garment spotted by the flesh.

—JUDE 23

May 9

Even the best of Bible teachers are only men and may fail you, but our Lord never will; and, if you trust Him, He will help you to discern the errors of men. —TBC

In hope of eternal life, which God, that cannot lie, promised before the world began; But hath in due times manifested his word through preaching, which is committed unto me according to the commandment of God our Saviour.

—TITUS 1:2,3

May 10

As our works had nothing to do in earning salvation, how dare we presume that our works are what keep us? Rather, as Ephesians 2:10 tells us, we are "created in Christ Jesus unto good works, which God hath before ordained that we should walk in them." In other words, we have a job to do. Let's get busy doing what we are called to do! —TBC

Wherefore, my beloved, as ye have always obeyed, not as in my presence only, but now much more in my absence, work out your own salvation with fear and trembling.

—PHILIPPIANS 2:12

May 11

We have seen how the Lord has used women mightily in unique ways in Old Testament times (Deborah, Abigail, Esther, and Rahab, to name a few); He continues to do so. Though Galatians 3:28 tells us that our *position* in Christ Jesus is neither male nor female (for we are all equal in Him), our *condition* is that God has created different spiritual as well as physical functions for us as human beings. The role of women is one of great importance and much to be sought after by those who understand its significance and value in the Kingdom (for example, 1 Timothy 3:11; 5:10; 6:1–2). I like what Paul said about Phoebe: that she was a succourer [help in time of need] of many, including himself (Romans 16:1–2). What a marvelous tribute! –TBC

And she said, I will surely go with thee: notwithstanding the journey that thou takest shall not be for thine honour; for the LORD shall sell Sisera into the hand of a woman. And Deborah arose, and went with Barak to Kedesh.

—JUDGES 4:9

May 12

How far may one deviate from the gospel? Simply speaking, if one's doctrine interferes with the gospel to the point where it begins to replace it, that line has been crossed. To teach that one must speak in tongues to be saved or that one's baptism plays a role in salvation is to go too far. May God cause us to adhere to the truth of the Scriptures: faith alone in Christ alone. To add anything to this is to ruin it. –TBC

Have all the gifts of healing? do all speak with tongues? do all interpret?

—1 Corinthians 12:30

May 13

The vows we made when we were wed are viewed seriously in God's sight, regardless of how lightly they are regarded by the world (and increasingly so by the church). Psalm 15 begins by asking who shall abide in the Lord's tabernacle and who shall dwell in His holy hill. Verse 4 answers, "He that sweareth to his own hurt, and changeth not." In other words, he that gives an oath or takes a vow and then doesn't change, even though it costs him, is someone who is worthy to abide in the Lord's tabernacle. –TBC

If a man vow a vow unto the LORD, or swear an oath to bind his soul with a bond; he shall not break his word, he shall do according to all that proceedeth out of his mouth.

—NUMBERS 30:2

May 14

A thorough familiarity with the Bible will show not only that Christians are responsible to admonish one another daily but also that most of the New Testament was of a corrective nature, that Paul rebuked Peter before them all, and Peter willingly accepted and was corrected by this, and that anyone who teaches publicly is and must be subject to public correction. –TBC

But when Peter was come to Antioch, I withstood him to the face, because he was to be blamed.

—GALATIANS 2:11

May 15

Too many issues that afflict the church began with those who sought for "the prophet" instead of following the example of the Bereans, who "searched the scriptures daily, [to see] whether these things were so" (Acts 17:11). –TBC

When a prophet speaketh in the name of the LORD, if the thing follow not, nor come to pass, that is the thing which the LORD hath not spoken, but the prophet hath spoken it presumptuously: thou shalt not be afraid of him.

—DEUTERONOMY 18:22

May 16

Isn't it interesting that whenever man takes liberties with the biblical account and begins speculating, the final product is a diminishing of the Word of God? —TBC

Not giving heed to Jewish fables, and commandments of men, that turn from the truth.

—Titus 1:14

May 17

Forget messages alleging to be from angels. The Scriptures warn us concerning the devil and his tactics. Second Corinthians 11:13–15 reveals that one of the adversary's favorite roles is to present himself as an angel of light. Paul further warned us in Galatians 1:8 that, "though we, or an angel from heaven preach any other gospel unto you than that which we have preached unto you, let him be accursed." –TBC

I marvel that ye are so soon removed from him that called you into the grace of Christ unto another gospel: Which is not another; but there be some that trouble you, and would pervert the gospel of Christ.

—Galatians 1:6–7

May 18

It is true that we are new creations in Christ (2 Corinthians 5:17) and that old things are passed away and all things are become new. It is also clear, however, that we are accountable for the choices we have made in the past. The prisoner who comes to the Lord must still serve out his sentence. The debtor must still repay his physical debts, and the father of children is still responsible for them, whether married to their mother or not. What has been wiped clean is our debt of sin and the judgment that hung over our heads (Colossians 2:14). The consequences of past failures may now be addressed with the confidence of a new creation. –TBC

Therefore if any man be in Christ, he is a new creature: old things are passed away; behold, all things are become new.

—2 Corinthians 5:17

May 19

Elijah did not hear God in the wind, the fire, or the earthquake, but he did hear Him—and powerfully—in the still, small voice. Scripture does exhort us to speak to each other in psalms, hymns, and spiritual songs. We do not praise and worship through someone else's lips—only through our own. In some instances, it seems that worship has become a spectator sport. I believe a caution is in order, but you must be the judge of these things for yourself. –TBC

And he said, Go forth, and stand upon the mount before the LORD. And, behold, the LORD passed by, and a great and strong wind rent the mountains, and brake in pieces the rocks before the LORD; but the LORD was not in the wind: and after the wind an earthquake; but the LORD was not in the earthquake: And after the earthquake a fire; but the LORD was not in the fire: and after the fire a still small voice.

—1 KINGS 19:11,12

May 20

Too many people who specialize in bleakness are held by a web of their own manufacture. To be obsessed with one's feelings is hardly an honest expression of humanity and is often just self-aggrandizement: "Look at me, see how pitiful I am!" Yes, this world is full of pain, disappointment, and sorrow unimaginable, but that does not mitigate our responsibility to maintain an objective (Christ-centered) rather than a subjective (self-centered) faith. —TBC

Wherefore seeing we also are compassed about with so great a cloud of witnesses, let us lay aside every weight, and the sin which doth so easily beset us, and let us run with patience the race that is set before us, Looking unto Jesus the author and finisher of our faith; who for the joy that was set before him endured the cross, despising the shame, and is set down at the right hand of the throne of God.

—HEBREWS 12:1–2

May 21

If we are totally depraved and can make no choice to do good, then this world would be hell, with unmitigated evil rampant! Yet there are plenty of examples of people who sacrifice their comfort, time, money, and even their lives to help others. All through the Bible, God pleads with sinners to repent—with Israel to obey Him; Jesus weeps over Jerusalem and says "How often would I…[but] *ye* would not" (Luke 13:34). All of this would be a mockery if, at the same time that God is pleading with men to repent, He is withholding from them the irresistible grace without which Calvin said man could not repent. The Bible clearly teaches that we have the right and power to choose—either to obey God or to disobey, to love or to hate, to accept the pardon for sin and eternal life (which He offers in His grace), or to reject it. –TBC

O Jerusalem, Jerusalem, which killest the prophets, and stonest them that are sent unto thee; how often would I have gathered thy children together, as a hen doth gather her brood under her wings, and ye would not!

—Luke 13:34

May 22

When we first become believers, it is often frustrating to see how little we seem to understand. Recognizing our lack of understanding is good, provided we take steps to move beyond it. How can we study the Bible and get the truth—not our own *understanding* of the truth? As you diligently read, study, and seek to obey God's Word, the Holy Spirit will cause your understanding to grow in the truth of the Scriptures. The more you grow in understanding, the easier it will be to recognize teachings that are not consistent with sound doctrine. The process is self-correcting, helping your own misunderstandings as well as the erroneous teachings of others. It will also help you to confidently glean more from those whom God has gifted to be teachers of His Word. –TBC

Thy word is a lamp unto my feet, and a light unto my path.

—PSALM 119:105

May 23

Matthew 7:8–11 tells us to seek. It's instructive also to consider Jeremiah 29:13: "And ye shall seek me, and find me, when ye shall search for me with all your heart." The key is repentance, something lacking in the professing church. We are told that the divorce rate of the American church is now the same as that of the world. What does this tell us about the state of repentance in the church? It is true that many are fasting and praying. However, Paul in I Corinthians 13:1–3 addresses the futility of "empty" sacrifice. There is a "seeking after God," but much of it is not wholehearted and, considering the low level of scriptural knowledge, much is not according to God. May God revive all of us in His way and in His time. –TBC

For every one that asketh receiveth; and he that seeketh findeth; and to him that knocketh it shall be opened.

—Matthew 7:8

May 24

Lack of doctrinal concern in favor of the experiential is perhaps the greatest problem within charismatic groups. A primary example would be a lack of scriptural discernment. This is perhaps best evidenced by the acceptance of the validity of the Charismatic Renewal of the Catholic Church, which Catholic leaders have claimed has enriched their participation in Catholicism, including the Sacraments and their devotion to Mary. With an exaltation of experience over the Scriptures, it is not surprising to see sound doctrine disparaged. –TBC

Beloved, believe not every spirit, but try the spirits whether they are of God: because many false prophets are gone out into the world.

—1 John 4:1

May 25

Forgiveness and grace are for those who truly have turned from sin to Christ and who don't want to sin and thus dishonor Him, but who may possibly fall into sin and, having done so, repent from their hearts. –TBC

If we confess our sins, he is faithful and just to forgive us our sins, and to cleanse us from all unrighteousness.

—1 John 1:9

May 26

When the Lord shares His heart and mind with us on something, it becomes, first and foremost, a basis for prayer. Oh, that we would find more Christians on their knees, praying with discernment and prophetic insight, with the mind of Christ! From that position, not only may we see changes (in situations, others, and ourselves) but, aware of what God is doing, we become the advance contingent, announcing His works through our praise—and often we ourselves will be given creative and unique opportunities to participate in the action. –TBC

Withal praying also for us, that God would open unto us a door of utterance, to speak the mystery of Christ, for which I am also in bonds.

—COLOSSIANS 4:3

May 27

The main things you must do are to study the Word of God, spend much time in communion with the Lord, and find a group of real Christians with whom you can fellowship regularly and who will hold you up in prayer and help you to grow in Christ. —TBC

Brethren, if a man be overtaken in a fault, ye which are spiritual, restore such an one in the spirit of meekness; considering thyself, lest thou also be tempted. Bear ye one another's burdens, and so fulfil the law of Christ.

—GALATIANS 6:1–2

May 28

When one's alleged "revelation knowledge" conflicts with God's Word, it is but a short step from this to cultism. We must never let visions, revelation, or any other experience supersede the scriptures (2 Peter 1:18–20). –TBC

Beloved, believe not every spirit, but try the spirits whether they are of God: because many false prophets are gone out into the world.

—1 John 4:1

May 29

Every Christian must stand before the judgment seat of Christ, where he shall suffer loss or gain reward. Paul referred to this experience as "terror" and used it as motivation for greater service (see also 1 Corinthians 3:10–15). The writer of Hebrews warned that the Lord chastened those who were His sons. Furthermore, the Bible states that those who are without correction are really not His children. Consequently, anyone who professes to be a Christian and appears to continue in sin demonstrates that he very likely is not one at all. –TBC

For we must all appear before the judgment seat of Christ;
that every one may receive the things done in his body,
according to that he hath done, whether it be good or bad.

—2 Corinthians 5:10

May 30

The Lord has His own time schedule and purposes for you, and He's the One who knows best how to equip you. Focus your attention on what you already know the Lord has shown you to do. It's amazing how, when we do what we already know we're to do, the Lord completes our understanding by giving us further answers. —TBC

A man's heart deviseth his way: but the LORD directeth his steps.

—PROVERBS 16:9

May 31

There are lasting values to consider that are far more important than temporary pleasure. This is true even for the unsaved person who has some ethical standards. What about honor and commitment? What about promises that have been made? In the long run, we would find lasting and deeper satisfaction and genuine joy at having been true to our commitments and having obeyed God and His Word, having kept our promises, and having lived for truth and honor. How could any temporary pleasure make up for the lasting regret one would have at knowing that honor and truth and commitment and righteousness had been trampled? –TBC

LORD, who shall abide in thy tabernacle? who shall dwell in thy holy hill? He that walketh uprightly, and worketh righteousness, and speaketh the truth in his heart.

—PSALM 15:1–2

June

June 1

The Bible is full of people who were hated, rejected, despised, abused, cast out even by their families, who suffered deprivation of all kinds, and yet who rejoiced in the Lord and triumphed in the faith. I find no hint that those mentioned in the last part of Hebrews 11 who were tortured, who wandered about in sheepskins and goatskins, destitute, tormented, afflicted, were able to pull through because they found someone who could minister deep emotional healing in the area of past abuses or rejection. It was simply a matter of faith in God, which comes from knowing Him—who He is, not who we are. –TBC

Thou wilt keep him in perfect peace, whose mind is stayed on thee: because he trusteth in thee.

—Isaiah 26:3

June 2

Baptism is a declaration to the world of an individual's acceptance of Jesus Christ as personal Savior—a visible demonstration of an invisible occurrence, in which the person has died to sin, is identified with Christ in His death, and is born to a new and living hope, thus also identifying with Christ in His resurrection. In the New Testament we see that people were baptized *after* they were saved. –TBC

Therefore we are buried with him by baptism into death: that like as Christ was raised up from the dead by the glory of the Father, even so we also should walk in newness of life.

—Romans 6:4

June 3

We know from Scripture that all things are lawful for us, but all things do not build up or strengthen us. Paul wrote that it was perfectly permissible for believers to partake of food offered to idols. After all, an idol was nothing when compared to the only true God. Nevertheless, in chapters 8 and 10 of 1 Corinthians, Paul lists some exceptions where our liberty must give way in consideration of others; and many places in Proverbs tell us how to occupy our time. The Bible has something to say about vain imaginations, as well. It tells us in Philippians what we should be thinking about. The Bible tells us how we are to live. –TBC

And that from a child thou hast known the holy scriptures, which are able to make thee wise unto salvation through faith which is in Christ Jesus.

—2 Timothy 3:15

June 4

Without exception, the Scriptures teach accountability in a local setting (i.e., elders) and personal accountability to God himself in an emphatic voice. With this in mind, individualism is far more preferable to the growing attitudes we see today. More and more Americans are acquiring the mindset needed for submission to a tyrannical spiritual authority. There is very little difference between surrendering your will and initiative to a political tyranny or to a spiritual one. –TBC

Continue in the faith grounded and settled, and be not moved away from the hope of the gospel.

—COLOSSIANS 1:23

June 5

Can you imagine the Apostle Paul proposing a Temple to be built in Rome to show the oneness of all the pagan religions with Christianity and that they really all worship the same God? What happened to the false gods? What happened to the idea that Satan deceives people with a false gospel and to Paul's exhortation that if anyone preaches another gospel, let him be accursed? We must resist all attempts to build places where any religious beliefs will be honored, no matter how false, and where the impression will be given that it doesn't matter what you call your God or what path you take so long as you are religious and sincere! The worst thing a person can have is a religious experience that is not from God, which then insulates them from the truth. —TBC

Take heed to thyself that thou be not snared by following them, after that they be destroyed from before thee; and that thou enquire not after their gods, saying, How did these nations serve their gods? even so will I do likewise.

—DEUTERONOMY 12:30

June 6

Mary has no power to do anything for me, and I don't need her, because Christ, who is God and who has all power, loves me infinitely. He has paid the complete debt of my sins so I don't have to be purged in purgatory. —TBC

For there is one God, and one mediator between
God and men, the man Christ Jesus.

—1 TIMOTHY 2:5

June 7

As I understand the Bible, man's problem is not that he cannot understand the gospel, nor that God does not desire everyone to be saved and does not do all He can to draw everyone to Himself, but that many *will not come* to Christ. Their refusal is such that no part of it is due to any failure by God to do all that He can to win every person by His love and grace. He has indeed made full provision for all to be saved through our Lord Jesus Christ. —TBC

And refused to obey, neither were mindful of thy wonders that thou didst among them; but hardened their necks, and in their rebellion appointed a captain to return to their bondage: but thou art a God ready to pardon, gracious and merciful, slow to anger, and of great kindness, and forsookest them not.

—NEHEMIAH 9:17

June 8

Is there a literal hell with literal flames? The Bible indicates that there is. Are those flames physical—or something even more horrible? Must something be physical to be real? Are the soul and spirit real? The rich man said he was "tormented in this flame" and asked that Lazarus might "dip the tip of his finger in water, and cool my tongue" (Luke 16:24). There was literal flame and burning thirst. Was it physical, or worse? His physical body was decaying in the grave and only his soul and spirit were in hell. —TBC

And they shall go forth, and look upon the carcases of the men that have transgressed against me: for their worm shall not die, neither shall their fire be quenched; and they shall be an abhorring unto all flesh.

—ISAIAH 66:24

June 9

Romans 10:9: "That if thou shalt confess…the Lord Jesus…thou shalt be saved." If Jesus is not God, He cannot save us, and if He is God (which He surely is), then He is Lord. No one can receive Christ as Savior and not as Lord, since He *is* Lord. A Jesus who is only Savior but not Lord is another Jesus. Christ doesn't become Lord, nor do we make Him Lord—He is Lord. Jesus doesn't come in two pieces: one of them Lord, the other Savior. –TBC

And Thomas answered and said unto him, My Lord and my God.

—John 20:28

June 10

The Bible tells us we are to run the Christian race "looking unto Jesus..." (Hebrews 12:2), not looking unto a picture or statue. Thus the problem with having a manmade focal point is that our imperfect concepts can often give the wrong impression of who Christ really is. Further, there is a danger of going beyond representation to an actual link with God. That's the purpose of pagan or Catholic shrines. They are a Power Point, so to speak. Catholics go to Lourdes or Fatima to be healed; pagans go to shrines and temples to offer sacrifices and seek their gods' favor. It is interesting that the Scriptures include the story of a man who was lying helpless beside one of these shrines but who found healing only when he met Jesus. –TBC

He answered and said, A man that is called Jesus made clay, and anointed mine eyes, and said unto me, Go to the pool of Siloam, and wash: and I went and washed, and I received sight.

—John 9:11

June 11

As it is beyond human capacity to comprehend the full nature of God's being, so man cannot understand his own being—what it means for him or anything else to exist—nor can we comprehend what space is or what time is or what matter is. The universe itself is an enigma: for every door science opens, there are ten more unopened doors on the other side. As one philosopher of science has said, the more we learn, the more rapidly the unknown expands before us like receding images in a hall of mirrors. We will never discover its ultimate secret by examining the universe itself—for all that we learn points beyond to its Creator! –TBC

Where was thou when I laid the foundations of the earth? declare, if thou hast understanding.

—Job 38:4

June 12

The Apostle Paul very carefully made some distinctions in 1 Corinthians 8:4–6: "We know…there is none other God but one. For though there be that are called gods…but to us there is but one God, the Father. . . ." He then acknowledges that there "is not in every man that knowledge…" (1 Corinthians 8:7). The Lord, who is knowledge, emphatically declares, "Before me there was no God formed, neither shall there be after me" (Isaiah 43:10) and "I am the LORD, and there is none else, there is no God beside me…" (Isaiah 45:5). –TBC

Talk no more so exceeding proudly; let not arrogancy come out of your mouth: for the LORD is a God of knowledge, and by him actions are weighed.

—1 SAMUEL 2:3

June 13

As far as God's justice is concerned, Abraham asked a pointed rhetorical question of the Lord: "Shall not the Judge of all the earth do right?" (Genesis 18:25). David wrote in Psalm 19 of the faithfulness of God in leaving a witness of Himself: "The heavens declare the glory of God; and the firmament sheweth his handiwork. Day unto day uttereth speech, and night unto night sheweth knowledge. There is no speech nor language, where their voice is not heard." So many scriptures speak of God's absolute justice and absolute love. Therefore, we can know that God is absolutely fair and just. As the Apostle Paul explained, "For the invisible things of him from the creation of the world are clearly seen, being understood by the things that are made, even his eternal power and Godhead; so that they are without excuse" (Romans 1:20). We do not know all the workings of God's justice and mercy, but we know enough from the Scriptures to realize that the Judge of all the earth will do that which is right. –TBC

That be far from thee to do after this manner, to slay the righteous with the wicked: and that the righteous should be as the wicked, that be far from thee: Shall not the Judge of all the earth do right?

—Genesis 18:25

June 14

Too often the phrase "Touch not God's anointed!" is an excuse for not exercising the discernment God has given us. Many who say this are unaware that they have already judged an individual to be a prophet of God and, as a consequence, will not do anything that might seem to question their statements or activities, no matter what they say or do. May God keep us from such fatal complacency. –TBC

Beloved, believe not every spirit, but [test] the spirits whether they are of God: because many false prophets are gone out into the world.

—1 JOHN 4:1

June 15

It is blatantly dishonest to attempt to explain away differences in belief by saying that they simply represent Progressive Revelation, when, in fact, they represent different "revelations" that contradict each other—and, therefore, cannot possibly all come from God, who does not contradict today what He said yesterday. It may sound unifying to declare that Truth is one but called by different names. That, however, ignores the fact that Truth involves definite concepts—the correct answers to life's ultimate questions—universal and timeless answers that do not change or vary with individuals or cultures. Greater revelation may be given, and has been given down through history as the Bible was being written, but the added revelations must agree with those of the past. You cannot build upon a foundation by undermining it. –TBC

Remember them which have the rule over you, who have spoken unto you the word of God: whose faith follow, considering the end of their conversation. Jesus Christ the same yesterday, and to day, and for ever. Be not carried about with divers and strange doctrines.

—HEBREWS 13:7–9

June 16

If there is no moral response possible on man's part, then "choose you this day" (Joshua 24:15) is impossible. –TBC

And if it seem evil unto you to serve the LORD,
choose you this day whom ye will serve; whether the gods
which your fathers served that were on the other side of the
flood, or the gods of the Amorites, in whose land ye dwell:
but as for me and my house, we will serve the LORD.

—JOSHUA 24:15

June 17

The worst kind of attack is an *ad hominem* one, wherein the character of your opponent is impugned and doubt is cast on his integrity, while the evidence he brings is avoided. As a debate teacher once said many years ago, "If your opponent immediately jumps to name calling, he's none too sure of his evidence." –TBC

Having a good conscience; that, whereas they speak evil of you, as of evildoers, they may be ashamed that falsely accuse your good conversation in Christ.

—1 PETER 3:16

June 18

The ministry of self-esteem is based upon a false foundation. It is only one of hundreds of conflicting psychological theories and thus is opposed by thousands of psychologists/psychiatrists both Christian and non-Christian. Moreover, it conflicts with God's Word (Philippians 2:3): "In lowliness of mind let each esteem other better than themselves," and Romans 12:3, which warns us not to think too highly of ourselves. Never does the Bible warn us not to think too *little* of ourselves, because we don't have that problem. Yet that, according to "Christian psychologists," is the cause of nearly every evil plaguing mankind today. Unfortunately, such teaching is not drawn from the Bible but from humanistic psychology. –TBC

For no man ever yet hated his own flesh; but nourisheth and cherisheth it, even as the Lord the church…

—EPHESIANS 5:29

June 19

Forget your identity! What matters is your relationship to Christ. Not who you are, but who He is; not what you are to Him, but what He is to you. Forget yourself. Stop trying to establish your identity, and turn your eyes upon Him alone. "Who I am in Christ" is another psychological term that comes from currently popular selfisms. It is not found in the Bible. You are nothing. He is everything. "He must increase, but I must decrease," said John the Baptist. John was not suffering from an identity crisis. This idea comes from humanistic psychology, not from the Bible, and it is tragic that Christians would fall for it. –TBC

And be found in him, not having mine own righteousness, which is of the law, but that which is through the faith of Christ, the righteousness which is of God by faith.

—PHILIPPIANS 3:9

June 20

The disciples turned the world upside down, but it was by preaching the gospel, not through political/social activism and public protest demonstrations. Preaching converts men's hearts—it does not pressure individuals or society into obeying God's laws. –TBC

And when they found them not, they drew Jason and certain brethren unto the rulers of the city, crying, These that have turned the world upside down are come hither also.

—Acts 17:6

June 21

Concerning the phrase "ye are gods" from Psalm 82, the individuals written of are those rulers of the earth whom God has ordained to rule. This accords with Romans 13:1–2, where the earthly authorities are identified as higher powers "ordained of God. Whosoever therefore resisteth the power, resisteth the ordinance of God. . . ." Clearly, God has placed into positions of power (Psalm 75:6–7) fallible men who will enforce the law and enable others to live in as much safety and peace as this world offers. As fallible men, many of them begin to take their authority as an excuse for considering themselves higher or better than others (i.e., as "gods"). God in turn brings them back to earth by pointing out the sure judgment that will come to them, "But ye shall die like men, and fall like one of the princes" (Psalm 82:7). —TBC

I have said, Ye are gods; and all of you are children of the most High. But ye shall die like men, and fall like one of the princes.

—Psalm 82:6–7

June 22

The Scriptures are silent for the most part as to whether children have an age of accountability beyond which they are lost if no repentance occurs. David could speak with certainty of where his son would be (2 Samuel 12:23), and Paul spoke of the believing parent sanctifying the children (1 Corinthians 7:14). Jesus admonished His disciples to "suffer little children to come unto me, and forbid them not: for of such is the kingdom of heaven" (Luke 18:16–17). He spoke of the childlike attitude a believer was to have and left us with a strong implication that a sizeable portion of heaven's population is made up of children (i.e., those who died as children). —TBC

But Jesus called them unto him, and said, Suffer little children to come unto me, and forbid them not: for of such is the kingdom of God. Verily I say unto you, Whosoever shall not receive the kingdom of God as a little child shall in no wise enter therein.

—LUKE 18:16–17

June 23

Not all that appears to the human senses as a miracle proves to be one. –TBC

Even him, whose coming is after the working of Satan with all power and signs and lying wonders...

—2 THESSALONIANS 2:9

June 24

There is nothing in the Bible to indicate that no matter how one dies (for example, in an explosion or, as in Hebrews 11, if sawn in half) the Lord would have any difficulty whatsoever in resurrecting our bodies. "I am the Lord; is anything too hard for me?" –TBC

Is any thing too hard for the LORD? At the time appointed I will return unto thee, according to the time of life, and Sarah shall have a son.

—GENESIS 18:14

June 25

The Apostle's Creed is an example of how men take the Word of God and the things of the Spirit and make a formula with which others may agree. Of these, however, too many give lip service without considering what the words actually mean. –TBC

This people draweth nigh unto me with their mouth, and honoureth me with their lips; but their heart is far from me.

—MATTHEW 15:8

June 26

It is clear that "belief" and not "baptism" is the criteria for salvation. Baptism does not save, yet throughout the book of Acts we see converts submitting to water baptism. Jesus Himself was baptized, stating "thus it becometh us to fulfill all righteousness" (Matthew 3:15). –TBC

Can any man forbid water, that these should not be baptized, which have received the Holy Ghost as well as we?

—Acts 10:47

June 27

The Lord calls us from many backgrounds and cultures; we all bring our baggage with us, having the mistaken idea that "this is who we are." But this is nonsense. No one has to put on an extensive wardrobe in "order to be me." –TBC

But by the grace of God I am what I am: and his grace which was bestowed upon me was not in vain; but I laboured more abundantly than they all: yet not I, but the grace of God which was with me.

—1 CORINTHIANS 15:10

June 28

Humanity has always had a fascination with fairy tales, myths, and legends. Paul spoke about those who were weak and thus susceptible to occult influences (1 Corinthians 8:6–13). Therefore, if certain types of fiction feed someone's imagination, then it is better that they be avoided. —TBC

For if any man see thee which hast knowledge sit at meat in the idol's temple, shall not the conscience of him which is weak be emboldened to eat those things which are offered to idols?

—1 CORINTHIANS 8:10

June 29

As good stewards, even when things seem impossible we should act responsibly. As far as possible, without disobeying God we should follow those in authority over us. This, by definition, would include being subject to the government we currently have. –TBC

Let every soul be subject unto the higher powers. For there is no power but of God: the powers that be are ordained of God. Whosoever therefore resisteth the power, resisteth the ordinance of God: and they that resist shall receive to themselves damnation. For rulers are not a terror to good works, but to the evil. Wilt thou then not be afraid of the power? do that which is good, and thou shalt have praise of the same.

—Romans 13:1–3

June 30

The creation (and that includes man) declares the glory of the God who created it, not the worth of self. You may respect your own body and being, but only in the same sense that you respect everything else that God made. That is not self-esteem/respect. Self has caused man to come short of God's glory and has marred God's creation (in himself as well as around him). This is cause for repentance and sorrow and humility, not for having a high regard (esteem/respect) of self. —TBC

For all have sinned, and come short of the glory of God.

—Romans 3:23

July

July 1

It makes no more sense for a man than for a mirror to attempt to develop a positive self-image! As C.S. Lewis put it, we are mirrors whose brightness, if we are bright, is wholly derived from the sun that shines upon us. No basis for self-esteem/respect/worth in that! –TBC

So God created man in his own image, in the image of God created he him; male and female created he them.

—Genesis 1:27

July 2

Why do we sin? Because we are not infinite in wisdom and thus can be deceived by Satan, sin, and our own lusts. It was inevitable that Adam and all of his offspring should sin. But God had made provision for that before He created man. Why do some accept salvation and others reject it? That is the mysterious nature of free will. –TBC

But every man is tempted, when he is drawn
away of his own lust, and enticed.

—JAMES 1:14

July 3

In contrast to that of Muhammad, Buddha, et al., who could only offer codes of ethics, Christ's perfect life condemns all mankind and shows that we are sinners who cannot possibly live up to God's standards. Moreover, Christ did what none of the founders of the world's other religions claimed to do or even dared attempt: He died for our sins and rose from the grave in triumph over death. Christ's grave is empty—the graves of all of the others are occupied and may be visited by their followers. –TBC

Knowing that Christ being raised from the dead dieth no more; death hath no more dominion over him.

—ROMANS 6:9

July 4

How do we plant a seed? According to some televangelists, we send money! This is a typical "seed-faith" scheme. Over and over the appeal is to personal gain, something that has been a consistent feature of many cults, pseudo-Christian groups, and word-faith churches. We need to pray that the Lord will give discernment to distinguish the false from the true. –TBC

Perverse disputings of men of corrupt minds, and destitute of the truth, supposing that gain is godliness: from such withdraw thyself.

—1 TIMOTHY 6:5

July 5

The issue is God's truth vs. Satan's lie. I believe in miracles, but I also believe that God primarily does miracles out of love and compassion in order to meet needs rather than to persuade the unsaved to believe in Him. –TBC

But I tell you of a truth, many widows were in Israel in the days of Elias, when the heaven was shut up three years and six months, when great famine was throughout all the land; But unto none of them was Elias sent, save unto Sarepta, a city of Sidon, unto a woman that was a widow.

—Luke 4:25–26

July 6

We do not serve a cruel God who demands too much. Paris Reidhead, a missionary in Africa for two decades, stated that his motive for going to Africa was that he felt that no one should go to hell without having heard the name of Jesus. After he got to Africa and had spent some time among the people, he found that they had a far more sophisticated concept of the Most High God than he would have suspected. They had an amazing awareness of sin, freely confessed that they were monsters of iniquity, and continued to serve their tribal deities because they had convinced themselves that the Most High God had given up on them! It is a mistake to say that people don't know better. —TBC

For the invisible things of him from the creation of the world are clearly seen, being understood by the things that are made, even his eternal power and Godhead; so that they are without excuse.

—Romans 1:20

July 7

We do not have to have a pastor to be saved, to receive the Holy Spirit's guidance, to pray, to communicate, or to read the Word with understanding. The Holy Spirit is our ultimate teacher, as John tells us in his first epistle (1 John 2:27). Certainly, the Lord has given the church teachers (Ephesians 4:11), but if their teaching begins to contradict the Word of God, then we must conclude that there is something wrong and act in obedience to the Holy Spirit, who convicts our hearts. —TBC

But the anointing which ye have received of him abideth in you, and ye need not that any man teach you: but as the same anointing teacheth you of all things, and is truth, and is no lie, and even as it hath taught you, ye shall abide in him.

—1 John 2:27

July 8

The Thessalonians of Acts 17 did not reject the message of Christ because of *sola scriptura*. They rejected the message Paul brought them for the same reason the religious leaders of Israel rejected Jesus. The Thessalonians rejected the gospel because they did not believe the words of Scripture. They did not deliberate for three weeks and decide that Paul's words contradicted the Torah; they simply refused to believe, because the words of Scripture clashed with their tradition. —TBC

Do not think that I will accuse you to the Father: there is one that accuseth you, even Moses, in whom ye trust. For had ye believed Moses, ye would have believed me: for he wrote of me. But if ye believe not his writings, how shall ye believe my words?

—JOHN 5:45–47

July 9

It is one thing to say that everyone is united in their belief that the Cross of Jesus Christ is the primary focus of their faith, but it is something else to define what this means. Even Mormons and Jehovah's Witnesses would agree with that, and certainly Roman Catholics would, but in fact, their teaching about the Cross will send those who believe it to hell. —TBC

Beware of false prophets, which come to you in sheep's clothing, but inwardly they are ravening wolves.

—MATTHEW 7:15

July 10

How willing are we to give up material things—even things we feel are necessary, not merely ornamental—in order to give a good witness to others, to support the Lord's work, to demonstrate to Him that we desire to please Him in all things? For effective witnessing, can we afford the appearance of self-indulgence? I think of the Scripture that tells us to abstain from even the appearance of evil (I Thessalonians 5:22) and this is meant so as not to weaken our witness to others. –TBC

Yea doubtless, and I count all things but loss for the excellency of the knowledge of Christ Jesus my Lord: for whom I have suffered the loss of all things, and do count them but dung, that I may win Christ.

—PHILIPPIANS 3:8

July 11

It takes courage, patience, longsuffering, and grace to be vulnerable as we reach out to others who don't yet have a lot of discernment. It may be that God would have us in a church to serve Him in helping the immature. If everyone in the Body were doing what God has called them to do, the unsaved would be more receptive to the Gospel and the saved who are still childish and haven't shed the secular would mature more quickly. On the other hand, the Lord may lead us abruptly out of a place. When we can totally trust Him for guidance and wait for His timing, and then obey His leading, we can know with confidence that we are where He wants us to be. –TBC

And the servant of the Lord must not strive; but be gentle unto all men, apt to teach, patient…

—2 Timothy 2:24

July 12

You received salvation by simply receiving it, knowing how unworthy you were; you receive all the rest of your Christian life the same way, knowing how unworthy you still are. It's grace, grace, grace! –TBC

For I know that in me (that is, in my flesh,) dwelleth no good thing: for to will is present with me; but how to perform that which is good I find not.

—Romans 7:18

July 13

Ephesians 5:18 tells us that we are not to be "drunk with wine, wherein is excess; but be filled with the Spirit…" in contrast to the flesh. The issue here is control. As wine to a certain degree controls us and influences our actions, we in contrast must be filled with the Spirit. The Holy Spirit then becomes that which prompts our praying, singing, and blessing. The Scriptures continually urge us to consider the example of the Lord Jesus Christ, who did everything in submission to and dependence upon His Father (John 5:19; 8:28; 14:10). –TBC

And be not drunk with wine, wherein is excess; but be filled with the Spirit; Speaking to yourselves in psalms and hymns and spiritual songs, singing and making melody in your heart to the Lord.

—Ephesians 5:18–19

July 14

We can understand why we have trials and afflictions by reading the Word of God. We can relate to the experiences of the writers of the Psalms, who went through great trials and were strengthened in the process. The writer of Psalm 119 confessed that "before I was afflicted, I went astray: but now I have kept thy word" (verse 67). And who hasn't received encouragement from the book of Job? –TBC

So then faith cometh by hearing and
hearing by the word of God.

—Romans 10:17

July 15

The Holy Spirit indwells us from the moment of salvation (Romans 8:9; 1 Corinthians 12:13). Second Peter 1:3–8 tells us that we have been given all things that pertain unto life and godliness. The newly inducted soldier is given his uniform, helmet, rifle, pack, inoculations, and everything that pertains to his life as a soldier. Does that mean that he immediately uses everything with soldierly proficiency? Of course not! He needs training, he needs to build familiarity, and he needs experiences that cause him to use efficiently what he has been given. This is much like the Christian life. —TBC

And the things that thou hast heard of me among many witnesses, the same commit thou to faithful men, who shall be able to teach others also.

—2 TIMOTHY 2:2

July 16

If you have fallen into the habit of wringing your hands over your failure and inability, and if in the back of your mind you think that this somehow excuses you, please understand something. It does not. It is now time for you to rise up as a soldier of the Cross, put on the whole armor, and go out to fight the good fight of faith in total reliance upon the One who has called you, who has promised to be with you and give you His victory. Stop concentrating on your weaknesses and failures and look instead to Him. Fall in love with Him afresh because of who He is and what He has done. You need to turn from your own inadequacies and trust God. —TBC

And the LORD said unto Joshua, Get thee up; wherefore liest thou thus upon thy face? Israel hath sinned, and they have also transgressed my covenant which I commanded them: for they have even taken of the accursed thing, and have also stolen, and dissembled also, and they have put it even among their own stuff.

—JOSHUA 7:10–11

July 17

Regardless of whether someone claims faith in Christ, the only way to know whether or not they are saved is *not* on the basis of a past decision (one's memory could be faulty) but on whether they are willing to let Christ be Lord of their lives right now in the present. If not, then it is likely that they never were saved—not that they had lost their salvation. –TBC

For we are his workmanship, created in Christ Jesus unto good works, which God hath before ordained that we should walk in them.

—EPHESIANS 2:10

July 18

The practice of necromancy, or contact with the dead, is consistently forbidden by the Scriptures. Consider King Saul's sad fate as just one example. In the Book of Isaiah, the prophet spoke of the abomination of seeking contact with the spirit world. Under the inspiration of the Holy Spirit, he called it rebellious and a way that is not good (65:2), iniquity and blasphemy (v. 7). He further rebukes the ones: "Who sit among the graves, and spend the night in the tombs" (v. 4). Every scriptural indication is that the place of the righteous dead is a place of comfort, a place apart from the cares of this world. Samuel specifically rebuked Saul for disturbing his peace (I Samuel 28:15). –TBC

Regard not them that have familiar spirits, neither seek after wizards, to be defiled by them: I am the LORD your God.

—LEVITICUS 19:31

July 19

"Come out from among them and be *ye* separate" may mean leaving a group, but ultimately it means *your* personal separation unto God and must be understood in the context of not only separating oneself from worldly things but also going with the gospel and *your* demonstration of Christ in your life into all the world—even the world that is, sadly, found also in the churches. –TBC

Wherefore come out from among them,
and be ye separate, saith the Lord, and touch not
the unclean thing; and I will receive you.

—2 Corinthians 6:17

July 20

Those who have been drawn by Christ (who is engaged in drawing all men—John 12:32) yet have not yielded to Him may temporarily "escape" the pollution of the world (Scripture doesn't say they have escaped the judgment) by an outward conformity based on head knowledge. But as Scripture plainly states, that conformity is not real, because their true nature (as a dog or pig) soon manifests itself. –TBC

For if after they have escaped the pollutions of the world through the knowledge of the Lord and Saviour Jesus Christ, they are again entangled therein, and overcome, the latter end is worse with them than the beginning.

—2 PETER 2:20

July 21

Many have the idea that prophecy is limited to foretelling events of the future. According to Paul, he who "prophesies speaks unto men to edification, exhortation, and comfort." A study of the entire Bible will show numerous examples of people prophesying who were doing such things as playing instruments and singing. How many of us in the course of listening to a Bible-inspired hymn or chorus have been edified, exhorted, and comforted? All this requires gifting from the Lord. —TBC

But he that prophesieth speaketh unto men to edification, and exhortation, and comfort.

—1 Corinthians 14:3

July 22

To the one without Christ, or the one whose relationship with Christ is marred by infatuation with self, the "lies, deceit, wars, murder, wickedness in high places, political chicanery," etc., will certainly wear them down. Why shouldn't it? And if you look to other Christians—again, we aren't to use them as our standard. As Christians, we are not to be of this world. –TBC

For we wrestle not against flesh and blood, but against principalities, against powers, against the rulers of the darkness of this world, against spiritual wickedness in high places.

—Ephesians 6:12

July 23

We should seek the Lord's direction daily. No greater advice can be given than, "Trust in the LORD with all thine heart; and lean not unto thine own understanding. In all thy ways acknowledge him, and he shall direct thy paths" (Proverbs 3:5–6). And again, "Commit thy way unto the LORD; trust also in him; and he shall bring it to pass" (Psalm 37:5). In other words, don't run ahead of the Lord. Don't ask the Lord to use you; ask Him to make you usable. –TBC

In all thy ways acknowledge him,
and he shall direct thy paths.

—PROVERBS 3:6

July 24

We know from 1 Corinthians 10:13 that all temptations (including homosexuality) can be forsaken and that God has provided a way of escape. Paul had already noted this in 1 Corinthians 6:11. The Scriptures do not support speculation that a tendency toward a particular sin is the same as being born a full-fledged practitioner of it. No child born to a line of drunkards is born a drunkard. The weaknesses and temptations are there, but choices are also there all along the way. The issue is not whether a person is born that way, but that there is a way whereby we may change. –TBC

There hath no temptation taken you but such as is common to man: but God is faithful, who will not suffer you to be tempted above that ye are able; but will with the temptation also make a way to escape, that ye may be able to bear it.

—1 Corinthians 10:13

July 25

Some have turned the biblical model of God upside down. Experience is sought over the revealed will of God. The scriptural model is to seek God, and then you will have experiences. Instead, a group of people has arisen who rush from one alleged "hot spot" to another and differ little from the inhabitants of Mars Hill who "spent their time in nothing else, but either to tell, or to hear some new thing" (Acts 17:21–22). —TBC

Now Peter and John went up together into the temple at the hour of prayer, being the ninth hour.

—ACTS 3:1

July 26

To share the compassion of Jesus is indeed the bottom line for all of us. As Romans 12:8 makes clear, one person may share and communicate that love through service; another, through mercy, giving, administration, exhortation, prophecy, and so on. One way the world will know that we are His (John 17:20–23) is when every member of the Body understands and fulfills his own function or role and understands and encourages the roles of others about him, for this is truly working together in unity. –TBC

From whom the whole body fitly joined together and compacted by that which every joint supplieth, according to the effectual working in the measure of every part, maketh increase of the body unto the edifying of itself in love.

—EPHESIANS 4:16

July 27

Because man has the power of choice (without which there is no real obedience, love, etc.), there is a genuine battle for man's heart and soul—and Satan is allowed to do his best. God has not stacked the deck or tied Satan's hands behind his back. –TBC

And if it seem evil unto you to serve the LORD, choose you this day whom ye will serve; whether the gods which your fathers served that were on the other side of the flood, or the gods of the Amorites, in whose land ye dwell: but as for me and my house, we will serve the LORD.

—JOSHUA 24:15

July 28

The ever-changing whim of man is no substitute for the eternal certainty of the Scriptures. —TBC

Jesus answered and said unto them, Ye do err, not knowing the scriptures, nor the power of God.

—MATTHEW 22:29

July 29

The Bible is not a "promise book," as some present it. All Scripture is spiritually discerned (I Corinthians 2:14). It is the Holy Spirit who directly applies specific verses to our condition. We do not have the right to randomly snatch passages of Scripture and insist that they apply to our particular situation. –TBC

But the natural man receiveth not the things of the Spirit of God: for they are foolishness unto him: neither can he know them, because they are spiritually discerned.

—1 CORINTHIANS 2:14

July 30

We may not understand the "why" of our troubles, but we know from the Scriptures that there is a reason. Second Corinthians 12 very plainly states that God allowed Satan to buffet Paul, and Paul specifically asked God three times to remove his affliction, with God's reply that "my grace is sufficient for thee" (2 Corinthians 12:9). Regardless of what we think or what our tradition may teach us, this was God saying no to Paul and explaining that the affliction had a specific purpose and was a necessary protection for him (2 Corinthians 12:7). –TBC

And lest I should be exalted above measure through the abundance of the revelations, there was given to me a thorn in the flesh, the messenger of Satan to buffet me, lest I should be exalted above measure.

—2 Corinthians 12:7

July 31

The Bible itself is the best resource on praise and the Lord Himself is the One who, when we know Him, generates it within our hearts: "Make a joyful noise unto the LORD, all ye lands. Serve the LORD with gladness: come before his presence with singing. Know ye that the LORD he is God: it is he that hath made us, and not we ourselves; we are his people, and the sheep of his pasture" (Psalm 100:1–3). –TBC

Enter into his gates with thanksgiving, and into his courts with praise: be thankful unto him, and bless his name. For the LORD is good; his mercy is everlasting; and his truth endureth to all generations.

—PSALM 100:4–5

August

August 1

True Bereanship does not allow us to fall into categorical thinking of any kind that then forces us to ignore some facts in order to justify our position. This, of course, jars those who need or prefer more structured forms of thought, and it removes some of the comfort zones we all, as human beings, tend to want. –TBC

But sanctify the Lord God in your hearts: and be ready always to give an answer to every man that asketh you a reason of the hope that is in you with meekness and fear.

—1 Peter 3:15

August 2

Proverbs 27:17 tells us that as "Iron sharpeneth iron; so a man sharpeneth the countenance of his friend." With this in view, we don't need to worry about criticizing "God's man" when we share a divergent opinion, as long as our confrontation follows the biblical admonition of gentleness and patience. –TBC

And the servant of the Lord must not strive; but be gentle unto all men, apt to teach, patient, in meekness instructing those that oppose themselves; if God peradventure will give them repentance to the acknowledging of the truth.

—2 TIMOTHY 2:24–25

August 3

With so many appropriating the word "global," it's not surprising that Christian groups have also latched onto the word and applied it to what may be a perfectly legitimate mission project. The call to "unity" that we hear so loudly these days is certainly something to be concerned about, and many of these so-called Christian "global" efforts are only a tool for ecumenism. At the very least, so many like-sounding groups will certainly cause confusion. How much we need to hold to the Lord's admonition to "prove all things, hold fast that which is good" (I Thessalonians 5:21)! —TBC

As ye have therefore received Christ Jesus the Lord, so walk ye in him: rooted and built up in him, and stablished in the faith. . . . Beware lest any man spoil you through philosophy and vain deceit, after the tradition of men, after the rudiments of the world, and not after Christ.

—COLOSSIANS 2:6–8

August 4

We are warned that all of the true children of the Lord will be corrected. The Lord does not take his disobedient children lightly and points out that judgment begins at His house (I Peter 4:17). As to repentance, it is clear that the process of believing involves a turning (repentance) from our dead works. Paul spoke of how he testified both to the Jews and Gentiles, "repentance toward God and faith toward our Lord Jesus Christ" (Acts 20:21). He reminded the Thessalonians that they had "turned to God from idols (or repented) to serve the living and true God" (I Thessalonians 1:9). It is no different today. –TBC

For whom the Lord loveth, he chasteneth, and scourgeth every son whom he receiveth.

—HEBREWS 12:6

August 5

There is no perfect Christian school—in fact, so-called Christian colleges have led multitudes astray. The only hope is for your children to be thoroughly grounded in God's Word and to know why they believe what they believe before they go off to college. –TBC

And thou shalt teach them diligently unto thy children, and shalt talk of them when thou sittest in thine house, and when thou walkest by the way, and when thou liest down, and when thou risest up.

—DEUTERONOMY 6:7

August 6

Proving things out of the Qur'an when witnessing to Muslims would be basing your discussion on faulty ground. Instead, you have the Word of God, and even though Muslims believe it's been perverted, we know that God's Word is powerful. It's like a hammer smashing rocks; it does what it's sent to do, never returns void, and goes directly to the heart of a matter. –TBC

Is not my word like as a fire? saith the LORD; and like a hammer that breaketh the rock in pieces?

—JEREMIAH 23:29

August 7

In this age, the emphasis is often on a nonoffensive, nonconfrontational gospel, but such a gospel is disobedient to the command of Christ (Matthew 28:19–20). –TBC

Preach the word; be instant in season, out of season; reprove, rebuke, exhort with all long suffering and doctrine.

—2 TIMOTHY 4:2

August 8

The Scriptures are clear on the matter of womanly subjection, both in a church context and in relation to her husband. In keeping with the order that the Lord has established, women are not to pastor churches, teach, or otherwise be in authority over men (I Corinthians 11:3; I Corinthians 14:33–35,40; Ephesians 5:21–33; I Timothy 2:12; I Peter 3:1–7). They may, however, teach other women (Titus 2:3,5) and pray or prophesy in the church (I Corinthians 11:5). –TBC

Wives, submit yourselves unto your own husbands, as it is fit in the Lord.

—Colossians 3:18

August 9

What do we do to work the works of God? I'll stick with the Lord Jesus' answer: "This is the work of God, that ye believe on him whom he hath sent" (John 6:29). That's what it means to obey Him (Hebrews 5:8–9). If someone says that believing is a work, apparently they haven't thought that statement through. The crowd that followed Jesus around was expecting an answer much as this: teach and baptize others, attend worship with church, remain faithful, pray, etc. But Jesus' actual answer was truly astounding. None of the preceding expectations were correct. All were meritorious, but none had anything to do with initiating our salvation. This reveals the basic error that those of a works-mentality perpetuate. Belief is our foundation; works follow those who are truly saved. We can't put the cart before the horse. To do so is to set oneself up for legalistic frustration and ultimate failure. –TBC

But it is good for me to draw near to God: I have put my trust in the Lord GOD, that I may declare all thy works.

—PSALM 73:28

August 10

Can a Christian be unforgiving? Certainly—but it is a serious thing to harbor such an attitude. –TBC

But if ye do not forgive, neither will your Father which is in heaven forgive your trespasses.

—MARK 11:26

August 11

First John 2:24–26 says in part, "Let that therefore abide in you, which you have heard from the beginning. . . ." This passage was intended to prevent us from being led astray. We can trust our God to equip and guide us in unique and solid ways—as He wills, in His time, for His purposes. In the meantime, it is important to pursue what we already know. It's interesting that when we are diligent about the things we do know to do, the Lord provides further insights. –TBC

A man's heart deviseth his way:
but the LORD directeth his steps.

—PROVERBS 16:9

August 12

We are well aware that there are many (and increasing) manifestations of icons sweating oil (or tears, or blood), and of oil or blood dripping from people's hands, but that does not mean these are from the Lord. This can be (a) the result of chicanery (human manipulation and fraud) or (b) a demonic manifestation—in either event, meant by Satan to deceive. The final word is found in the Scriptures. The Lord has warned against icons; see Exodus 20:4. He has warned that in the last days, some shall give heed to seducing spirits and doctrines of devils (1 Timothy 4:1), seducers shall wax worse and worse, deceiving, and being deceived (2 Timothy 3:13), false prophets shall rise and show signs and wonders to try to seduce even the elect (Mark 13:22), and people will no longer endure sound doctrine, but turn away their ears from the truth unto fables (2 Timothy 4:3–4). –TBC

And they shall turn away their ears from the truth, and shall be turned unto fables.

—2 Timothy 4:4

August 13

Anyone who builds a doctrine on one or two verses has taken a step along a road to an undesired destination. –TBC

As also in all his epistles, speaking in them of these things; in which are some things hard to be understood, which they that are unlearned and unstable wrest, as they do also the other scriptures, unto their own destruction.

—2 PETER 3:16

August 14

Concerning those who cast out demons, we as Christians do have authority to do this, but it is not a practice we should undertake without the guidance of the Holy Spirit. To minister deliverance to a person without the Holy Spirit's specific instruction can be very harmful (Acts 19:13–16, Luke 11:24–26). —TBC

And the evil spirit answered and said, Jesus I know, and Paul I know; but who are ye?

—Acts 19:15

August 15

What difference is there between God commanding the Israelites to kill the inhabitants of the Promised Land and those today who believe it is their "god's" will for them to take other people's land? Consider one obvious difference—God *told* the Israelites to do so; the others *imagine* the same. In addition, the Lord gave the inhabitants of Canaan more than 400 years to repent, but He eventually came to the point where He had to stop the unending sacrifice of infants and institutional outpouring of blood (Genesis 15:13–16). –TBC

But thou shalt utterly destroy them; namely, the Hittites, and the Amorites, the Canaanites, and the Perizzites, the Hivites, and the Jebusites; as the LORD thy God hath commanded thee.

—DEUTERONOMY 20:17

August 16

We have no way of knowing all the simplest ways the Lord can use us to minister His life to others. Often we pray for ministry, but when the Lord gives the opportunity, we don't recognize it, as it's so different from what we had in mind. In fact, it may be distasteful and demand much of us and keep us on our knees. Especially the latter—how we need intercessors in the churches today! –TBC

Then shall he answer them, saying, Verily I say unto you, Inasmuch as ye did it not to one of the least of these, ye did it not to me.

—MATTHEW 25:45

August 17

We must never let the abuses and distortions of some folks keep us from receiving from Him through the genuine "Ephesians 4" ministries that Christ has given to His church. May God encourage us in these days. –TBC

And he gave some, apostles; and some, prophets;
and some, evangelists; and some, pastors and teachers;
For the perfecting of the saints, for the work of the
ministry, for the edifying of the body of Christ...

—EPHESIANS 4:11–12

August 18

Eve was deceived and sinned, but Adam was not deceived. Adam sinned with his eyes wide open. —TBC

And Adam was not deceived, but the woman being deceived was in the transgression.

—1 Timothy 2:14

August 19

When we are highly visible Christians in positions of leadership and influence, yet are communicating and facilitating wrong doctrine, not only are we going to be held even more accountable to God (James 3:1; I Corinthians 4:1,2) but we are to be corrected publicly (I Timothy 5:20). —TBC

Against an elder receive not an accusation, but before two or three witnesses. Them that sin rebuke before all, that others also may fear.

—1 Timothy 5:19–20

August 20

The repentance Jonah preached is not activism as advocated today. Jonah did not lead a protest march. No pagan empire was ever rebuked, as it is understood today. Neither were the prophets of Israel "Christian activists." Many a good application for today lies within the story of the Good Samaritan. He modeled a tremendous compassion, which is certainly worthy of emulation and indeed most desperately needed. But to call it "activism," particularly in the light of today's usage, is to obscure what the Holy Spirit is teaching. The Samaritan did not pursue the thieves—much less try to reform society. –TBC

But a certain Samaritan, as he journeyed, came where he was: and when he saw him, he had compassion on him. And went to him, and bound up his wounds, pouring in oil and wine, and set him on his own beast, and brought him to an inn, and took care of him.

—LUKE 10:33–34

August 21

There is no basis for self-esteem/respect, even if I obey and serve God perfectly, for it can only be through His grace and power and not of Self. Moreover, Christ said that if we do everything we are supposed to do, we must still regard ourselves as unprofitable servants who have done only what we ought to have done. In fact, we are less than that and thus have cause for shame as fallen creatures, not for self-respect or self-esteem or self-worth! —TBC

So likewise ye, when ye shall have done all those things which are commanded you, say, We are unprofitable servants: we have done that which was our duty to do.

—LUKE 17:10

August 22

If we were just pawns of our personalities, the passage below would lose meaning. Further, 1 Corinthians 10:13 specifically tells us that no one is tempted beyond their ability to resist. It must therefore follow that individuals have a conscious role to play in their decisions. —TBC

For we must all appear before the judgment seat of Christ;
that every one may receive the things done in his body,
according to that he hath done, whether it be good or bad.

—2 Corinthians 5:10

August 23

A review of the places where the Scriptures refer to "God hates" will evidence the fact that, whereas the Lord loves us, His children, it is not humanity that He hates but sin and iniquity. —TBC

Howbeit I sent unto you all my servants the prophets, rising early and sending them, saying, Oh, do not this abominable thing that I hate.

—JEREMIAH 44:4

August 24

It is a libel on the character of God to suggest that billions will go to hell simply because God didn't want them in heaven—not because I have made this judgment, but because the Bible itself tells me in the clearest of terms that God loves the whole world, He sent His Son to redeem the whole world, and He wants the whole world to be saved. All other verses about election must take this fact into account. –TBC

And he is the propitiation for our sins: and not for ours only, but also for the sins of the whole world.

—1 John 2:2

August 25

The "falling away" doctrine is another vestige from Rome, where, as you know, no one can tell you when enough Masses have been said, enough rosaries recited, enough indulgences earned to assure heaven—and salvation can always be lost. –TBC

My Father, which gave them me, is greater than all; and no man is able to pluck them out of my Father's hand.

—JOHN 10:29

August 26

Christ was gentle with those who had been deceived, but He sternly rebuked the rabbis who had perverted God's Word by false teaching—and He did so publicly. –TBC

The scribes and the Pharisees sit in Moses' seat: All therefore whatsoever they bid you observe, that observe and do but do not ye after their works: for they say do not. For they bind heavy burdens and grievous to be borne, and lay them on men's shoulders; but they themselves will not move them with one of their fingers.

—MATTHEW 23:2–4

August 27

We are being conditioned to accept witch doctors and sorcerers (yoga experts, acupuncturists, rolfers, iridologists, crystal gazers, and any number of other shamans) as health-care professionals. No matter what your physical condition is, let us encourage you to seriously consider your spiritual condition when you think you should resort, in essence, to witchcraft in order to get relief. —TBC

So Saul died for his transgression which he committed against the LORD, even against the word of the LORD, which he kept not, and also for asking counsel of one that had a familiar spirit, to enquire of it.

—1 CHRONICLES 10:13

August 28

Today, some are devoting the majority of their Sunday services to accommodating unbelievers. That is not the purpose of the church. It is one thing to have special evangelistic services to invite unbelievers to, but that is not a meeting of the church. –TBC

For when for the time ye ought to be teachers, ye have need that one teach you again which be the first principles of the oracles of God; and are become such as have need of milk, and not of strong meat.

—HEBREWS 5:12

August 29

Of more immediate help than a Bible college is to become part of a good Bible-based Christian fellowship where God's Word is taught without compromise and where mature Christian men can disciple and pray with you. It should be a place where you can grow in and demonstrate the mature handling of Scripture not only in word but in every aspect of your life; where you can learn to relate fully to the body of true believers in that fellowship and serve and minister and bless there in various ways, as the Lord makes your spiritual gifts apparent, first to them and then to yourself (you may be surprised)—all, so "that ye may prove what is that good, and acceptable, and perfect, will of God" (Romans 12:2). —TBC

Go ye therefore, and teach all nations, baptizing them in the name of the Father, and of the Son, and of the Holy Ghost: Teaching them to observe all things whatsoever I have commanded you: and, lo, I am with you alway, even unto the end of the world.

—Matthew 28:19–20

August 30

"Do all speak with tongues?" asks Paul. The response is obviously that not all speak in tongues any more than all are workers of miracles, etc. But the false teaching that all do, and the attempt to get all to speak in tongues, has introduced much error and even occultism into the Pentecostal/charismatic movement. Seek the Giver first of all, and receive from Him whatever gifts He bestows. Knowing Him and being crucified with Christ and experiencing His life being lived through you is the first priority. Get that right, and all else will fall into place. –TBC

Are all apostles? are all prophets? are all teachers? are all workers of miracles? Have all the gifts of healing? do all speak with tongues? do all interpret?

—1 Corinthians 12:29–30

August 31

Actual repentance (turning from sin) begins with a heart conviction quickened by the Holy Spirit of one's sin, a mental recognition and assent that one is a sinner, and a revulsion to that sin—a revulsion that may never before have existed. –TBC

But go ye and learn what that meaneth, I will have mercy, and not sacrifice: for I am not come to call the righteous, but sinners to repentance.

—MATTHEW 9:13

September

September 1

When we're obedient to all that we already know God clearly asks of us, He opens up our understanding further. We're to seek first the Kingdom of God and His righteousness (Matthew 6:33). He's in charge of our spiritual growth, its pacing, its sequence, its individual shaping and preparation for the purpose He has for each of us. We can trust Him fully. Someone has said, "He won't do our part, and we can't do His part." Instead of looking about at others, allow Him to grow you into the very special and individual person you were meant to be. –TBC

But seek ye first the kingdom of God, and his righteousness; and all these things shall be added unto you.

—Matthew 6:33

September 2

It isn't necessary (or often even beneficial) to join any denomination. You need to be associated with a local body of believers. In all denominations there are both good and bad congregations, depending upon the pastor and those who attend. Look for a group of believers in your area who love the Lord and who are seeking to be true to His Word. Don't expect perfection, and don't think primarily of what the church can do for you, but rather of what you can do to help others. –TBC

Let no corrupt communication proceed out of your mouth, but that which is good to the use of edifying, that it may minister grace unto the hearers.

—Ephesians 4:29

September 3

We believe that the spiritual gifts of I Corinthians flow from God through chosen human instruments at the time to meet needs as God wills and that no human instrument possesses these gifts, over which he then has total control or that he can use any time he pleases. —TBC

But now hath God set the members every one of them in the body, as it hath pleased him.

—1 CORINTHIANS 12:18

September 4

Bondage to anything brings out the worst in us, so to speak. That is, when something other than God becomes god in our lives, not only does He allow the natural consequences of our choices to take effect, but we're at the whim of our adversary, who can then give us an added push as our sins become rampant. –TBC

And the nation to whom they shall be in bondage will I judge, said God: and after that shall they come forth, and serve me in this place.

—ACTS 7:7

September 5

Tongues is the only gift that can be easily counterfeited. To those who uncritically accept any manifestation as from the Lord, the emphasis is then on experience rather than the unchanging Word of God. Peter pointed to a more sure word of prophecy—the Scriptures—rather than an experience, even that tremendous experience on the Mount of Transfiguration (2 Peter 1:16–21). —TBC

Knowing this first, that no prophecy of the scripture is of any private interpretation. For the prophecy came not in old time by the will of man: but holy men of God spake as they were moved by the Holy Ghost.

—2 Peter 1:20–21

September 6

The true church of God is not an organization; it is an organism. That is why the Scriptures refer to it as the body of Christ, and whenever the Scriptures address the concept of "the church" they are speaking of the individuals of which it is composed (1 Corinthians 3:9; 1 Corinthians 12:12, 27; Ephesians 2:21–22). –TBC

The churches of Asia salute you.
Aquila and Priscilla salute you much in the Lord,
with the church that is in their house.

—1 Corinthians 16:19

September 7

You and I both know many things that seem good for a while, even though they aren't biblical. Has not God been faithful and longsuffering and patient with us in spite of our woeful ignorance and lack? Someone dying of thirst may perhaps get some sustenance from a polluted stream, but if he continues to drink from it he will die. Instead, we have the crystal clear river of life. –TBC

And he shewed me a pure river of water of life, clear as crystal, proceeding out of the throne of God and of the Lamb.

—REVELATION 22:1

September 8

Consider Revelation 1:16 in a passage describing the awesome majesty of the Lord Jesus Christ. The narrative states that "out of his mouth went a sharp two-edged sword. . . ." We know that Jesus does not literally have a two-edged sword in His mouth. Nevertheless, with this image we are able to have some understanding concerning the authority and power by which our Lord and Savior speaks. This is complicated, however, by our limited understanding. As we read through the book of Revelation, there are some passages that are clearly literal, some that are clearly symbolic, and some that are difficult to judge. It would be good to remember the admonition of James: "If any of you lack wisdom, let him ask of God, that giveth to all men liberally, and upbraideth not…" (James 1:5). –TBC

And he had in his right hand seven stars: and out of his mouth went a sharp twoedged sword: and his countenance was as the sun shineth in his strength.

—Revelation 1:16

September 9

Regarding worship, is the mood of the music befitting the presence of the Lord, and is there moral, spiritual, and doctrinal content that convicts sinners, edifies worshipers, and exalts the Lord? The Scriptures tell us to test all things. Without straining at a gnat and swallowing a camel, we should consider whether or not music pleases the flesh more than it does our Savior. Does a particular song lead you to worship Him in spirit and in truth? Can you listen without doubt (anything done without faith is sin)? Is there false doctrine or heresy in the song? Is it worldly, ritualistic, purely emotional, unbiblical, raucous, impudent, or unholy? –TBC

The LORD is my strength and song, and he is become my salvation: he is my God, and I will prepare him an habitation; my father's God, and I will exalt him.

—EXODUS 15:2

September 10

It's so important to know the full counsel of God; otherwise, we're at the mercy of teachings that may not be taking into account all of the Scriptures, and may not be allowing Scripture to interpret Scripture. This is why TBC cares so much to help people become Bereans as they search out truth from God's Word day after day with all diligence. As we continue to read the Bible, we grow in discernment and are able to recognize error and false teaching when we hear it. –TBC

Study to shew thyself approved unto God,
a workman that needeth not to be ashamed,
rightly dividing the word of truth.

—2 Timothy 2:15

September 11

Because all are not pulling equally, some must bear a greater portion of the load. When it comes to correction, that load falls upon those who have been labeled "heresy hunters." This is a misnomer, as there is very little hunting involved. Most of the modern heresies are so blatant that one must react or else be overwhelmed. By the time the sewer backs up, it's past time to take action. –TBC

"For I mean not that other men be eased, and ye burdened."

—2 Corinthians 8:13

September 12

Don't be concerned as to who or how many are for a certain doctrine. Neither let those who are against it be the final authority. The real concern is, "What do the Scriptures say?" –TBC

Wherein they think it strange that ye run not with them to the same excess of riot, speaking evil of you.

—1 PETER 4:4

September 13

How can you best equip your children to resist anti-God teaching in the classroom? The most important thing is to be very sure your children are intimately acquainted with the truth. They need to know what the Scriptures alone teach if they are to have a foundation that will withstand the disruptive intrusions of man. –TBC

If thy children will keep my covenant and my testimony that I shall teach them, their children shall also sit upon thy throne for evermore.

—Psalm 132:12

September 14

There is no need to tell others how bleak the world is; they already know. We, on the other hand are to be "holding forth the word of life…" (Philippians 2:16). –TBC

In my Father's house are many mansions:
if it were not so, I would have told you.
I go to prepare a place for you.

—JOHN 14:2

September 15

None of His wonderful promises exclude women; not one of them has failed (1 Kings 8:56). We are to seek first the Kingdom, and His righteousness (Matthew 6:33). For the man or woman who is obedient to Christ, trusting only in Him, the Lord of hosts will open the windows of heaven and pour out such a blessing—more than we can receive (Malachi 3:10), pressed down, shaken together, overflowing (Luke 6:38), exceedingly abundantly above all that we can ask or think, according to the power that works in us (Ephesians 3:20). —TBC

Blessed be the LORD, that hath given rest unto his people Israel, according to all that he promised: there hath not failed one word of all his good promise, which he promised by the hand of Moses his servant.

—1 KINGS 8:56

September 16

The child of God need only recognize, repent, and confess that sin of which he is aware, and receive God's cleansing and forgiveness (I John 1:9). With that comes greater insight and, especially in cases of habitual sin, new awareness of sin—always with a further drawing back from it, as God removes the scales from our eyes and frees us in a process so simple that it's often ignored. –TBC

If we confess our sins, he is faithful and just to forgive us our sins, and to cleanse us from all unrighteousness.

—1 JOHN 1:9

September 17

Deuteronomy 22:5 does not mean women should wear only dresses and men, pants. It expresses a principle more basic than appears on the surface, in that God has created woman separate from man and given each a role to play, beginning with sexuality and procreation but including the order in a family. These roles include submission and headship, a separation unto one another in union, etc., and thus give a visible definition to the world of God's authority and our submission, His ordering of things, and most wonderfully, the concepts of Father and children, of Bridegroom and Bride, of spiritual faithfulness vs. spiritual adultery. When our clothing expresses a perversion of and rebellion against these definitions, we give a message against God and against the gospel. However, to take Deuteronomy 22:5 at face value only, and to make it a mere mechanical rule, would be to follow the letter rather than the spirit of the passage and to subvert the real meaning and truth of God's Word by legalism. God looks on the heart. —TBC

The woman shall not wear that which pertaineth unto a man,
neither shall a man put on a woman's garment:
for all that do so are abomination unto the LORD thy God.

—DEUTERONOMY 22:5

September 18

Though the prophets didn't fully understand it, Paul still calls it the gospel of God, which he had promised afore by his prophets in the holy Scriptures. One of the most powerful arguments that we have for Jews or anyone is the fact that the entire gospel, from Christ's birth to life to death and resurrection, was all foretold in detail in the Old Testament. We are simply preaching today what God has proclaimed in His Word for thousands of years! —TBC

Paul, a servant of Jesus Christ, called to be an apostle, separated unto the gospel of God, (Which he had promised afore by his prophets in the holy scriptures)...

—Romans 1:1–2

September 19

Many toys today reflect the demoralization of our society and the negative impact it makes upon children. The problem with some toys is not that they have demons in them but rather (a) are, in some cases, demonically inspired (knowingly or unknowingly) and (b) the conditioning effect they have in causing children to feel familiar and comfortable with strange beings or those that can cast spells, as well as (c) replacing time that could be spent on whatever is true, honest, pure, lovely, and of good report (Phil. 4:8) with a preoccupation with sinister, evil-looking, or frightening entities. Children identify rather strongly with their toy characters and thus through fantasy may be living out the life of the toy. Depending on the toy and what it stands for, this can be dangerous. Some of these toys are fairly innocuous. Others bear occult or other questionable or suggestive marks, symbols, or names. –TBC

Come, ye children, hearken unto me: I will teach you the fear of the LORD.

—PSALM 34:11

September 20

We are to trust the Scriptures above the pronouncement of any man or woman. In addition, the fact that someone quotes Scripture does not validate their ministry. It has been often pointed out that during the temptation in the wilderness, Satan quoted Scripture to the Lord (Matthew 4; Luke 4). One can point to several cults whose founders began receiving prophecies at a very early age. According to I Corinthians 14:3, the New Testament prophet "speaketh unto men to edification, and exhortation, and comfort." We certainly can use this kind of prophecy. Unfortunately, the natural bent of humanity is to look to those who profess to foretell the future instead of those who tell forth the Word of God. –TBC

To the law and to the testimony: if they speak not according to this word, it is because there is no light in them.

—Isaiah 8:20

September 21

Worship is much more than a special prayer time. There are many times when our heart may be so overwhelmed with the goodness of the Lord that we spontaneously worship Him. In Hebrews, referring to Jacob blessing the sons of Joseph, it is stated that he "worshipped, leaning upon the top of his staff" (Hebrews 11:21). At one time Jacob thought he would never see his son Joseph again, and now he was seeing Joseph's children, and he worshiped God. –TBC

By faith Jacob, when he was a dying, blessed both the sons of Joseph; and worshipped, leaning upon the top of his staff.

—HEBREWS 11:21

September 22

With respect to the argument that if any part of the Bible is less than 100 percent accurate then the whole Bible is under question and cannot stand as an absolute anchor of truth—it is not the Bible that is in question regarding accuracy; it is a particular translation and that only in very minor ways. There are certainly enough study materials, Greek/Hebrew interlinears, concordances, Bible dictionaries, commentaries, and thousands of extant manuscripts to help us reconcile the seeming discrepancies. Further, most of these do not come near major doctrines. We also tend to forget something else. The Scriptures are spiritually discerned. The Holy Spirit must teach us as we read them in order for understanding to take place (1 Corinthians 2:14). –TBC

The words of the LORD are pure words: as silver tried in a furnace of earth, purified seven times.

—PSALM 12:6

September 23

More than one commentator has pointed out that in modern America there are no more heroes. Thank God that we still have the unchanging witness of those who have gone before us and triumphed over hatred, peril, torment, persecution, and many other afflictions. May God encourage us with their examples. —TBC

And what shall I more say? for the time would fail me to tell of Gedeon, and of Barak, and of Samson, and of Jephthae; of David also, and Samuel, and of the prophets: Who through faith subdued kingdoms, wrought righteousness, obtained promises, stopped the mouths of lions…

—HEBREWS 11:32–33

September 24

We must always interpret experience by the Scriptures, not the other way around, and we dare not extrapolate supposed theories or principles from some impression or sensation. Read 2 Peter 1:18–20. Even after one of the greatest experiences anyone could have, Peter reminds us that the Word is "more sure." –TBC

Jesus answered and said unto them, Ye do err, not knowing the scriptures, nor the power of God.

—Matthew 22:29

September 25

Why won't there be another fall, and another, and another? Whereas the Holy Spirit initially left Adam when he sinned, Christ comes into our hearts never to leave. Thus the union between man and God that He establishes can't be broken. Christ's death in the past pardons even future sin. But His love has changed our hearts. We truly love Him and don't want to sin but to please Him, and He will make that possible by giving us new bodies not subject to lust or sin and by placing us in heaven where there will be no temptation. –TBC

Knowing this, that our old man is crucified with him, that the body of sin might be destroyed, that henceforth we should not serve sin. . . . If we be dead with Christ, we believe that we shall also live with him.

—ROMANS 6:6–8

September 26

Christ will continue to reveal Himself to us, and we will continue to reflect His character. As we do, whatever gift He wants to manifest through us for a particular occasion, or whatever way He wants to motivate, encourage, and fulfill us in spreading His love, or whatever gift He wants us to become to the Body, will be made known to those around us without particular emphasis and without recourse to hype, self-promotion, research, questionnaires, or inventories. –TBC

Having then gifts differing according to the grace that is given to us, whether prophecy, let us prophesy according to the proportion of faith.

—Romans 12:6

September 27

Some have the idea that we have the right to claim healing always from anything and that if one is sick, it's due to sin and/or a lack of faith. This leads to "miracle" services where no miracles from God take place, but a lot of people get excited—and some even think they're healed, only to find out the next day that they aren't. So they come back again to another miracle service; and on and on it goes, and the world looks on and ridicules, and they become a reproach to the Lord. –TBC

And many shall follow their pernicious ways; by reason of whom the way of truth shall be evil spoken of. And through covetousness shall they with feigned words make merchandise of you.

—2 Peter 2:2-3

September 28

According to Ephesians 4:11–13, there are five specific ministries given to the church "for the perfecting of the saints, for the work of the ministry, for the edifying of the body of Christ." It is evident that until the Lord returns, there will always be a need for this perfecting of the saints (Christians) and the edification of the Body. The passage itself states that these ministries will be in operation until "we all come in the unity of the faith, and of the knowledge of the Son of God, unto a perfect man, unto the measure of the stature of the fullness of Christ." This day has evidently not arrived. –TBC

Being confident of this very thing, that he which hath begun a good work in you will perform it until the day of Jesus Christ.

—Philippians 1:6

September 29

Self-denial is not that we are to exist in a vacuum but is to be put in the context of pleasing my Creator. Thus, it is living to Him instead of to self. And in putting others first, I am doing so in order to be a channel of His love and grace—and, at the same time, committing myself into His care. –TBC

And he said unto me, My grace is sufficient for thee: for my strength is made perfect in weakness. Most gladly therefore will I rather glory in my infirmities, that the power of Christ may rest upon me.

—2 Corinthians 12:9

September 30

Those who understand that Jesus Christ wants to be Lord of their lives will place themselves under submission to His loving authority and in line with His purposes and ask to be filled with His Holy Spirit, leaving no opportunity for the enemy's attacks to prosper. Full surrender to Jesus Christ! No amount of ritual or ceremony will ever free anyone. –TBC

But I keep under my body, and bring it into subjection: lest that by any means, when I have preached to others, I myself should be a castaway.

—1 CORINTHIANS 9:27

October

October 1

God has been merciful to each of us while we were still ignorant of many things (as we are yet today), and He has been patient and longsuffering beyond measure. One of the fruit of our lives in Christ is the development of patience, and we would do well to witness and help others with the compassion of Christ. —TBC

Put on therefore, as the elect of God, holy and beloved, bowels of mercies, kindness, humbleness of mind, meekness, longsuffering…

—Colossians 3:12

October 2

As to the source of any goodness in sinners: Jesus said in Matthew 19:17, "Why callest thou me good? There is none good but one, that is, God. . . ." God has placed a conscience in the heart of every man. When man follows that conscience, some good may result. In man, however, the only eternal good comes by a work of the Holy Spirit in those who are saved. –TBC

Which shew the work of the law written in their hearts, their conscience also bearing witness, and their thoughts the mean while accusing or else excusing one another.

—Romans 2:15

October 3

We are saved and cleansed by the blood of Christ—not by some of it being sprinkled upon our physical bodies or infused into our veins but because His blood was poured out in His sacrificial death for our sins upon the Cross. –TBC

For by one offering he hath perfected for ever
them that are sanctified.

—HEBREWS 10:14

October 4

Salvation is through faith alone, as witnessed by the Scriptures. "For by grace are ye saved through faith; and that not of yourselves: it is the gift of God: Not of works, lest any man should boast" (Ephesians 2:8–9). "Not by works of righteousness which we have done, but according to his mercy he saved us" (Titus 3:5). However, some attempt to create a conflict between James and Paul and have James 2:14–26 saying "not by faith alone, but by works also." On the contrary, it says that works should follow faith. "I will shew thee my faith by my works" (James 2:18). This agrees with Ephesians 2:10: "For we are his workmanship, created in Christ Jesus unto good works." If we are truly saved by faith, there should be visible works showing that our salvation is real. Otherwise, "faith without works is dead also" (James 2:26). –TBC

Therefore we conclude that a man is justified by faith without the deeds of the law.

—ROMANS 3:28

October 5

The brain is neither intelligent nor does it even think. It is merely the computer that the mind uses to control the body in order to interface with the physical universe. –TBC

For to be carnally minded is death; but to be spiritually minded is life and peace.

—Romans 8:6

October 6

God is one God, yet three distinct persons: Father, Son, and Holy Spirit. Notice all the scriptures that demonstrate interaction between the persons of the Godhead. The Son prays to the Father; the Father speaks to the Son; the Son sends the Holy Spirit, and many others too numerous to mention. How else can these verses be explained? –TBC

And the Holy Ghost descended in a bodily shape like a dove upon him, and a voice came from heaven, which said, Thou art my beloved Son; in thee I am well pleased.

—LUKE 3:22

October 7

Everyone may freely choose Christ. However, only God knows who will. No one is predestined to hell. As an illustration, Romans 9:9–13 speaks of Esau and Jacob. God knew the failure of Esau before the children were ever born. He also knew that Jacob was the one through whom He could accomplish His purpose. Consequently, He chose (loved) Jacob and rejected (hated) Esau. –TBC

And the LORD said unto her, Two nations are in thy womb, and two manner of people shall be separated from thy bowels: and the one people shall be stronger than the other people; and the elder shall serve the younger.

—GENESIS 25:23

October 8

If Freud, Jung, et al., are legitimate sources of God's truth, then so are Buddha, Marx, Mary Baker Eddy, et al. Christ's declaration, "You will know the truth and the truth will set you free" must now be read, "You will know part of the truth and be set partly free, but I can't set you fully free, because my Word only contains part of the truth, awaiting the day when Freud et al. will declare the rest of God's truth and set you fully free." —TBC

For such are false apostles, deceitful workers, transforming themselves into the apostles of Christ.

—2 Corinthians 11:13

October 9

In Matthew 16, Jesus didn't tell His disciples that the important thing was to discover who they were, but "Whom do men say that I the Son of man am?" and "Whom say ye that I am?" Never are we told to get to know ourselves, but to know Him; it is no more I but Christ; beholding as in a glass—not our own glory or discovering who we are—but, beholding Him, we become like Him; when we see Him, we shall be like Him—not because we have at last found out who we really are in Christ but because we will see Him as He is! –TBC

Beloved, now are we the sons of God, and it doth not yet appear what we shall be: but we know that, when he shall appear, we shall be like him; for we shall see him as he is.

—1 JOHN 3:2

October 10

As citizens of this nation, we presently can affect its course to a certain extent by voting prayerfully for the best candidate we can and participating with wisdom in various enterprises that do not compromise the gospel. As citizens of heaven, we realize that the only real hope for our nation lies with our Lord. –TBC

And they that know thy name will put their trust in thee: for thou, LORD, hast not forsaken them that seek thee.

—PSALM 9:10

October 11

Whenever we add another specific to what the Lord Jesus Christ has done, there is a danger of obscuring the simplicity of the gospel. –TBC

But I fear, lest by any means, as the serpent beguiled Eve through his subtilty, so your minds should be corrupted from the simplicity that is in Christ.

—2 CORINTHIANS 11:3

October 12

Why is Islam the fastest growing religion of today? 1) Those of its adherents who are more than nominal are very fervent, devoted, and zealous; 2) Its missionaries are backed by a tremendous number of petrodollars; 3) Many of its followers are in nations where people have no birth control and large families; but even under other conditions, reproduction is basic to its proliferation; 4) A Muslim's basic understanding is that the whole world is meant to be, even born to be, Islamic; and Islam is to be spread by word and by sword (by word if it is received well; by sword if not); 5) The extreme penalties for anyone who leaves Islam for another faith operate as a strong deterrent even for those who feel trapped in Islam or who desire to convert from it. –TBC

Thou lovest all devouring words,
O thou deceitful tongue.

—Psalm 52:4

October 13

We are saved by the death of Christ (Romans 5), who declared (John 19:30) on the Cross that it was finished; however, implicit in that act and that statement was the joy set before Him (Hebrews 12:2): the certain fact of His resurrection, and all that both His death and resurrection obtained for "whosoever will" of mankind. –TBC

And the Spirit and the bride say, Come. And let him that heareth say, Come. And let him that is athirst come. And whosoever will, let him take the water of life freely.

—REVELATION 22:17

October 14

Even the woman who is regarded as gifted in some area helpful to the Body of Christ, who limits herself to those areas outlined in the Bible, though it may for a time seem a waste and a denial of what God has given her, will find great blessing and marvelous opportunities that could never have been reached without this kind of obedience. –TBC

I will therefore that the younger women marry, bear children, guide the house, give none occasion to the adversary to speak reproachfully.

—1 Timothy 5:14

October 15

Although funerals have pagan aspects in many cultures, including our own, they can be tremendous opportunities for expressing the blessed assurance of the Christian and for sharing our faith. They can have a life-changing impact on unbelievers as they observe the unmistakable peace and even joy of Christians, and as they hear the message of the gospel. –TBC

And though after my skin worms destroy this body, yet in my flesh shall I see God.

—JOB 19:26

October 16

Few organizations or movements set out to deceive, but without the kind of attention to careful dividing of the full counsel of God, and true Bereanship on the part of actual or potential individual believers, it can happen. And this can happen to an individual believer as well, whether he or she is part of a movement or not. May that be a constant admonishment to each of us. Our real adversary is not people. –TBC

For we wrestle not against flesh and blood, but against principalities, against powers, against the rulers of the darkness of this world, against spiritual wickedness in high places.

—Ephesians 6:12

October 17

To imply that we are not to judge teachings, movements, and doctrines is to be disobedient to the clear scriptural admonition of the Lord. He has called each one of us to be a judge (Matthew 7:1–5; 1 Corinthians 5:12; 6:2–5; Jude 1–25). To accomplish this, our judgment must be based on the sure Word of God—not on the constantly shifting foundation of experience. –TBC

Prove all things; hold fast that which is good.

—1 THESSALONIANS 5:21

October 18

Much of today's music that passes for worship is sorely lacking in the fear of God. —TBC

The fear of the LORD is the beginning of wisdom: a good understanding have all they that do his commandments: his praise endureth for ever.

—PSALM 111:10

October 19

The book of Leviticus contains two series of prohibitions for a precise reason. Much of Leviticus (as well as Numbers and Deuteronomy) is given over to specific prohibitions that the nation of Israel was to observe as a "special people unto me." Whether these prohibitions concerned eating of particular foods, wearing of specific garments, or other ceremonial considerations, the Lord consistently told Israel that such were unclean [or abomination] (Leviticus 11:7, etc.). This is one kind of prohibition, clearly applicable to Israel. On the other hand, issues such as adultery, sorcery, child sacrifice, bestiality, incest, homosexuality, etc., are said to be abomination (period). Penalties against those who commit these things are assessed because of God's judgment (Leviticus 18:4). As to the punishment, Jesus' actions concerning the woman taken in adultery (John 8:3) show that the law of Israel is not enforced in today's day of grace. –TBC

And all that have not fins and scales in the seas, and in the rivers, of all that move in the waters, and of any living thing which is in the waters, they shall be an abomination unto you.

—LEVITICUS 11:10

October 20

The Bible makes it clear that Israel was in a unique relationship with God that did not pertain to Gentiles at all. That relationship involved: (1) the land of Israel; (2) the Law of Moses; and (3) that the Messiah would reign over Israel on the throne of David. None of these pertained to Gentiles (Leviticus 20:24–26, Psalm 147:19–20, etc.), nor do they pertain to the church, which is a new entity composed of both Jews and Gentiles who have a different relationship with God through Jesus Christ not based upon the Mosaic law. God's saving grace does not turn Gentiles into Jews, but makes of both a new man (Galatians 3:23–29, Ephesians 2:11–22). –TBC

Brethren, my heart's desire and prayer to God for Israel is, that they might be saved.

—Romans 10:1

October 21

There are Pentecostal and charismatic churches where there is balance, order, careful doctrine, and emphasis on the Scriptures rather than on experience. But, as with everything close to the heart of God, the adversary tries to pervert and discredit it. —TBC

Let all things be done decently and in order.

—1 CORINTHIANS 14:40

October 22

The Bible never says that we are born sinners. We become sinners by sinning. The Bible does say that by the choice of one man, Adam, sin entered into the world, and death by sin, for all have sinned (Romans 5:12). Adam's sin separated him from God, the Source of life, and his body began to die. As a result, all of his descendants inherited bodies subject to death—but they can't blame Adam, because they, too, have sinned. –TBC

For there is not a just man upon earth,
that doeth good, and sinneth not.

—ECCLESIASTES 7:20

October 23

Is it a sin to gamble? Although some may argue that gambling is not addressed by name, it is clear from Proverbs and other places within the pages of Scripture that the whole concept of gambling is opposed to God's order. The Lord Jesus spoke about a "faithful and wise steward" (Luke 12:42) and the Proverbs contain much about stewardship and faithfulness in the use of one's resources. –TBC

Moreover it is required in stewards,
that a man be found faithful.

—1 Corinthians 4:2

October 24

Romans 12 concludes with instructions that override any preoccupation with spiritual gifts, telling us that love is to be without dissimulation, that we are to prefer one another, to be diligent, fervent, joyful, patient, instant in prayer and practical service, and not wise in our own conceits. To repeat a well-worn phrase, are we worshiping the gift or the Giver? Why do we look outside the Scriptures for understanding? –TBC

Let love be without dissimulation.
Abhor that which is evil; cleave to that which is good.

—Romans 12:9

October 25

As Christians, we are not designed to live in a vacuum. We need encouragement and admonition from, and accountability to, others. You need to plug into a small group where you can develop relationships and be open with others. –TBC

How is it then, brethren? when ye come together, every one of you hath a psalm, hath a doctrine, hath a tongue, hath a revelation, hath an interpretation. Let all things be done unto edifying.

—1 Corinthians 14:26

October 26

Should one be involved in selling a given product? That depends upon whether or not the product is worth selling and is a good value at the price. One should not, however, in any case become obsessed with selling and success. Unfortunately, such obsession is often encouraged, and Christians often fall into such a desire for success for allegedly good reasons—for example, in order to earn money to support missionaries, or to retire and serve the Lord later—that the business becomes the passion of their lives and their spiritual life suffers. –TBC

And that ye study to be quiet, and to do your own business, and to work with your own hands, as we commanded you.

—1 THESSALONIANS 4:11

October 27

The Scriptures are consistent in urging believers to concentrate on the day in which we live and not worry about future issues. –TBC

But exhort one another daily, while it is called To day; lest any of you be hardened through the deceitfulness of sin.

—HEBREWS 3:13

October 28

Why should I give up the definite promise of God's Word to embrace the indefinite promise of Roman Catholicism, that sometime, someway, somehow, after much suffering and hard work and purging in purgatory, I will make it at last—but don't ask how much of anything, or how long it will take?! –TBC

We are confident, I say, and willing rather to be absent from the body, and to be present with the Lord.

—2 Corinthians 5:8

October 29

Only the Holy Spirit can convict and convert the soul—but He is pleased to use us as His instruments. What a responsibility and privilege! –TBC

Now then we are ambassadors for Christ, as though God did beseech you by us: we pray you in Christ's stead, be ye reconciled to God.

—2 Corinthians 5:20

October 30

God has the right to send us all to hell, because that is exactly what we deserve. But at the same time, the Bible says that He is not willing that any should perish but that all should come to acknowledgment of the truth. I honor God by taking Him at His Word: That He loves all mankind so much that He wants everyone to be saved, that He has made full provision for their salvation, and that He has done all that He could to bring them to heaven. —TBC

The Lord is not slack concerning his promise, as some men count slackness; but is longsuffering to us-ward, not willing that any should perish, but that all should come to repentance.

—2 PETER 3:9

October 31

The public teaching of false doctrine is not a transgression against one personally. Nor can it be corrected in any manner but the one in which it was taught—publicly. –TBC

Them that sin rebuke before all,
that others also may fear.

—1 Timothy 5:20

November

November 1

A false prophet is one who claims to hear from God and speaks forth what God says, but who, in fact, neither truly hears from God nor speaks what He says. –TBC

But evil men and seducers shall wax worse and worse, deceiving, and being deceived.

—2 TIMOTHY 3:13

November 2

A Doctor of Divinity once said that the Bible is fallible because it was written by a man. Yet it has been viciously attacked, libeled, and demeaned throughout history. It is precisely because it is *not* a man-generated document that such attacks have come. –TBC

For the word of God is quick, and powerful, and sharper than any twoedged sword, piercing even to the dividing asunder of soul and spirit, and of the joints and marrow, and is a discerner of the thoughts and intents of the heart.

—HEBREWS 4:12

November 3

The Christian psychologists' response to *sola scriptura* is, "Indeed not!" However, their extrabiblical source of truth is not, as was Rome's, the opinions of religious leaders but the theories of anti-Christian humanists, justified by the specious slogan, "All truth is God's truth," confusing God's truth with facts of nature. –TBC

And take not the word of truth utterly out of my mouth; for I have hoped in thy judgments.

—PSALM 119:43

November 4

The fact that Paul declared that he had fought a good fight, had finished his course, and fulfilled the ministry given to him by the Lord is evidence that social action was not on the agenda—and that, I believe, holds true today, since we are to follow his example. It is important to remember that Noah was "a preacher of righteousness," not a "protestor for righteousness." –TBC

For I am now ready to be offered, and the time of my departure is at hand. I have fought a good fight, I have finished my course, I have kept the faith.

—2 Timothy 4:6–7

November 5

Practitioners of religious systems have two choices. They can either repent of their traditions and believe Scripture, or they can relegate Scripture to a "sacred" but clearly second-place position. –TBC

But ye say, Whosoever shall say to his father or his mother, It is a gift, by whatsoever thou mightest be profited by me; And honour not his father or his mother, he shall be free. Thus have ye made the commandment of God of none effect by your tradition.

—MATTHEW 15:5–6

November 6

It is one of the unfortunate aspects of today's Christianity that if a person expresses a belief in certain doctrines, he is immediately presumed to embrace all sorts of other things. Isn't it ironic that one may believe in the security of the believer and be accused by Arminian-minded folks of being a Calvinist while simultaneously being branded an Arminian by Calvinists? How important it is to rightly divide the Word of truth (2 Timothy 2:15)—rather than to fall in with the accepted doctrines of a particular persuasion! Our lives are further complicated because the abuses of some have tinged words with meaning beyond their original intent. How comforting in these confusing times to know that the "foundation of God standeth sure," and "the Lord knoweth them that are his" (2 Timothy 2:19). –TBC

Study to shew thyself approved unto God, a workman that needeth not to be ashamed, rightly dividing the word of truth.

—2 TIMOTHY 2:15

November 7

In all the admonitions concerning communion, Paul was laying the stress upon the individual and making it a matter of conscience between him and God. Because of this, any enforcement of who may or may not partake of communion takes place within each individual. Knowing the power of God, would it not be incumbent upon us to ask the Lord to open the eyes of those who are taking communion unworthily? –TBC

But let a man examine himself, and so let him eat of that bread, and drink of that cup.

—1 Corinthians 11:28

November 8

One must determine to serve the Lord wherever He may take us. For the Christian, there is no distinction between a secular career and a "spiritual" career. –TBC

And whatsoever ye do, do it heartily,
as to the Lord, and not unto men.

—COLOSSIANS 3:23

November 9

No verse in the Bible specifically forbids a person of one race to marry another. The Bible itself speaks of only one race—the human race. Acts 17:26 tells us that God "hath made of one blood all nations of men for to dwell on all the face of the earth, and hath determined the times before appointed, and the bounds of their habitation." However, God has drawn a distinction between the saved and the lost: "Be not unequally yoked together with unbelievers: for what fellowship hath righteousness with unrighteousness?" (2 Corinthians 6:14). With respect to Israel, the Lord commanded Israel to make no marriages with other nations, as they were to be a special and distinct people for the purpose of God (Deuteronomy 7:3–4; 1 Kings 11:2; etc.). But these commands were strictly for Israel. –TBC

Can two walk together, except they be agreed?

—Amos 3:3

November 10

There is no hint that the wicked servant was frustrated with the evil of the other servants and therefore beat them and ate and drank with sinners in order to quell the pain of the disappointment he felt. This is a teaching that we dare not adopt for ourselves. It was because the servant thought that his Lord would not come back yet and he would later have time enough to straighten up that he engaged in such sins. That is what Christ clearly says—let us not read something else into it. –TBC

But and if that evil servant shall say in his heart, My lord delayeth his coming; And shall begin to smite his fellowservants, and to eat and drink with the drunken; The lord of that servant shall come in a day when he looketh not for him, and in an hour that he is not aware of.

—MATTHEW 24:48–50

November 11

From all my reading of history I do not recall a single instance of Billy Sunday leading a protest march through town to the local brewery, nor did he lead a boycott of taverns. Instead, he preached the gospel. —TBC

For our gospel came not unto you in word only, but also in power, and in the Holy Ghost, and in much assurance; as ye know what manner of men we were among you for your sake. And ye became followers of us, and of the Lord, having received the word in much affliction, with joy of the Holy Ghost.

—1 Thessalonians 1:5–6

November 12

The fact is that so-called Christian psychologists have borrowed not only the methods but also the content and the basic theories of man from secular humanism; and having dressed them up in biblical, or Christian, language, they have tried to pass them off as "Christian" counseling. —TBC

Beware of false prophets, which come to you in sheep's clothing, but inwardly they are ravening wolves.

—MATTHEW 7:15

November 13

If we can't distinguish between what is biblical and what is not biblical, then clearly we have lost our scriptural bearings and moorings. Such is the fruit of the church's embrace of psychology. –TBC

And they shall teach my people the difference between the holy and profane, and cause them to discern between the unclean and the clean.

—Ezekiel 44:23

November 14

Concerning John 20:23, one must read one's presuppositions into the verse to support the doctrine of papal authority. Further, the Lord Jesus says nothing about passing a supposed authority on to a select group of individuals. In fact, the Scriptures are consistent in testimony that only God can truly forgive sins (Luke 5:21). Finally, anything given to the apostles by the Lord is not exclusive to them. The Lord Jesus assured them that "he [everyone] that believeth on me, the works that I do shall he do also; and greater works than these shall he do; because I go unto my Father" (John 14:12). —TBC

Forasmuch as ye know that ye were not redeemed with corruptible things, as silver and gold, from your vain conversation received by tradition from your fathers...

—PETER 1:18

November 15

I have seen both positive and negative results in home churches. There is a danger of a strong personality dominating a home church and moving it into areas that appear cultic. On the other hand, I have seen groups who have been strengthened and encouraged by their experience. Peter wrote in I Peter 5:2–3 that the elders were to "feed the flock of God which is among you, taking the oversight thereof, not by constraint, but willingly; not for filthy lucre, but of a ready mind; neither as being lords over God's heritage, but being examples to the flock." —TBC

Let the elders that rule well be counted worthy of double honour, especially they who labour in the word and doctrine.

—1 Timothy 5:17

November 16

"Extreme" Pentecostalism involves any forms of Pentecostalism that go beyond the clear teaching of Scripture—for example, the idea that speaking in tongues is the necessary sign of being filled with the Holy Spirit or even of being saved. That is not biblical, and it tends to lead into further error, such as trying to teach people to speak in tongues because everyone must have this experience; or people trying and tarrying and straining to get this gift and coming under guilt because they don't have it, and then either turning away from the Lord altogether in disillusionment or faking it. There are probably millions faking it today. —TBC

For by one Spirit are we all baptized into one body, whether we be Jews or Gentiles, whether we be bond or free; and have been all made to drink into one Spirit.

—1 CORINTHIANS 12:13

November 17

As to tests to determine your spiritual gift, exercise caution. A Berean who seeks to know the Lord and to reflect His character does not need manmade methods to grow in Christlikeness. "Beloved...we know that, when he shall appear, we shall be like him; for we shall see him as he is" (1 John 3:2). A focus on spiritual gifts runs the risk of getting people's eyes off Jesus, the author and finisher of our faith, and onto self. –TBC

And God hath set some in the church, first apostles, secondarily prophets, thirdly teachers, after that miracles, then gifts of healings, helps, governments, diversities of tongues.

—1 Corinthians 12:28

November 18

Whatever sins you have ever committed, you didn't *have* to but *chose* to. When you stand before God someday, you certainly won't be able to excuse your actions either by saying, "I had to do it, because I was born a slave of sin," or "The devil made me do it." —TBC

Let no man say when he is tempted, I am tempted of God: for God cannot be tempted with evil, neither tempteth he any man: But every man is tempted, when he is drawn away of his own lust, and enticed.

—JAMES 1:13–14

November 19

The issue of believers limiting their diets is nothing new, as Paul notes in Romans (14:1–3). And although we are enjoined to avoid gluttony and similar sin, too many teach vegetarianism as a sign of spiritual maturity. Rather than vegetarianism, it would be more profitable to study what the Scriptures say about fasting. –TBC

Him that is weak in the faith receive ye, but not to doubtful disputations. For one believeth that he may eat all things: another, who is weak, eateth herbs. Let not him that eateth despise him that eateth not; and let not him which eateth not judge him that eateth: for God hath received him.

—ROMANS 14:1–3

November 20

Role-playing is similar to visualization. It can be a worthwhile technique but it can also be harmful. A basic yardstick in deciding its value is the content of the role-playing situation. Psalm 101:3 says, "I will set no wicked thing before mine eyes." If it's questionable or evil (playing a sorcerer, for instance, in Dungeons and Dragons, which is occult), the effect very likely will be spiritually destructive and even demonic. On the other hand, if the role-playing content has no particular moral consequences (for example, rehearsing a job interview with someone), it may prove very helpful. But role-playing games almost always include extreme violence, not mere intelligence, to be successful or to avoid destruction. –TBC

I remember the days of old; I meditate on all thy works; I muse on the work of thy hands.

—Psalm 143:5

November 21

God is preparing His people in little pockets here, little crevices there, through whom the world will yet know that we are God's chosen people, so that "if our gospel be hid, it is hid [only] to them that are lost" (2 Corinthians 4:3). —TBC

But what saith the answer of God unto him?
I have reserved to myself seven thousand men, who
have not bowed the knee to the image of Baal.

—Romans 11:4

November 22

Psychology erroneously attempts to explain human behavior in terms other than our sinfulness and moral accountability to God and turns sin into a mental disease or some unconscious urge caused by past traumas, etc. This is the trap that so-called Christian psychologists fall into continually. –TBC

For I know that in me (that is, in my flesh,) dwelleth no good thing: for to will is present with me; but how to perform that which is good I find not.

—Romans 7:18

November 23

If we are truly saved by faith, there should be visible works showing that our salvation is real. Otherwise, "faith without works is dead also" (James 2:26). –TBC

Yea, a man may say,
Thou hast faith, and I have works:
shew me thy faith without thy works, and
I will shew thee my faith by my works.

—JAMES 2:18

November 24

Paul asked this question of the Corinthians. We see in this passage a clear recognition of diversity, with a caution that the end must result in the edification of believers. The document seems to be an attempt to accommodate that diversity while maintaining the order. –TBC

How is it then, brethren? when ye come together, every one of you hath a psalm, hath a doctrine, hath a tongue, hath a revelation, hath an interpretation. Let all things be done unto edifying.

—1 Corinthians 14:26

November 25

The cumulative effects of sin, disease, and depravity working in mankind since the Garden of Eden have made us less wise and less intelligent than Adam, and certainly today's world is filled with far more temptations to sin than Eden was—but we have no more reason to sin than Adam. —TBC

Moreover the law entered, that the offence might abound. But where sin abounded, grace did much more abound: That as sin hath reigned unto death, even so might grace reign through righteousness unto eternal life by Jesus Christ our Lord.

—ROMANS 5:20–21

November 26

Just because God knows all that will happen before it happens does not mean that He therefore causes it to happen. He knew all of the sin that would occur on this planet, but He surely did not cause it! That He has allowed it we don't deny, but there is a big difference between causing and allowing. He likewise knows who will accept and who will reject His offer of grace, but He does not cause some to believe and others to reject—He allows men to reject if that is their decision. –TBC

Declaring the end from the beginning, and from ancient times the things that are not yet done, saying, My counsel shall stand, and I will do all my pleasure.

—Isaiah 46:10

November 27

Beware, then, of taking a simplistic approach to the failures of professing Christians today that explains it all in terms of unscriptural evangelistic methods (e.g., "easy believism") and denies that they are saved at all on the basis of their carnality. True, a false gospel is in many instances being preached, and there are false methods that produce false converts who are a plague in the church. Yet we dare not deny that "the flesh lusteth against the Spirit, and the Spirit against the flesh" (Galatians. 5:17). This is as true today as it was in the first century and will continue to be true of every Christian until the redemption of our bodies! —TBC

What then? notwithstanding, every way, whether in pretense,
or in truth, Christ is preached; and I therein
do rejoice, yea, and will rejoice.

—PHILIPPIANS 1:18

November 28

Paul preached the gospel, which is the power of God unto salvation to everyone who believes. He didn't first establish that there was a hierarchy that alone could interpret the Scriptures. When you preach to Hindus, does not the Holy Spirit take the Word of God and convict them and bring them to Christ? The Holy Spirit bears witness even in the hearts of unsaved that this is the truth of God! That is all we need—not some magisterium! –TBC

And on the sabbath we went out of the city by a river side, where prayer was wont to be made; and we sat down, and spake unto the women which resorted thither.

—Acts 16:13

November 29

The fear of man, or a desire to be well thought of by others or to gain some important or influential person's approval, has led many astray. We need to remember that one day we will give an account to Him. Time is so very short and eternity so long! –TBC

The fear of man bringeth a snare: but whoso putteth his trust in the LORD shall be safe.

—PROVERBS 29:25

November 30

As for the apparent contradictions regarding sinning in I John 1:8–10 and not sinning in 3:6–10, the only way these can be reconciled is if the latter doesn't mean falling into sin inadvertently now and then and repenting of it, but practicing sin, living in sin, and enjoying it as a way of life. In fact, that is what the Greek means. It doesn't mean that a real Christian never sins. John makes that clear in 2:1. "These things write I unto you, that ye sin not," tells us that the aim of the Christian is to live without ever sinning. That is God's will; it is possible, or else John would not hold it out as the standard. On the other hand, "and if any man sin, we have an advocate with the Father" tells us that it is also possible for a Christian to sin—and that sinning doesn't mean that he ceases to be a Christian, because he is still a child of the Father. –TBC

Whosoever abideth in him sinneth not: whosoever sinneth hath not seen him, neither known him.

—1 John 3:6

December

December 1

The only biblical base for being "slain in the spirit" is Ananias and Sapphira, who were killed by the Spirit because of their sin, and the Apostle John, who fell at the feet of Jesus as dead. A study of Scripture indicates that those under God's *judgment* fall backward (1 Samuel 4:18; John 18:6), whereas those touched by God's majesty fall on their faces (Genesis 17:3; Numbers 22:31; Joshua 5:14; 1 Kings 18:7; Matthew 26:39; Luke 5:12; 17:16 etc.). Nowhere in the Bible do we have men of God, either Old Testament prophets or New Testament apostles, going around touching people to make them fall down. But this is common among Hindu gurus and is called the *shaktipat*, meaning the "force touch" (Shakti is Kali, consort of Shiva, the "Star Wars Force" of Hinduism). –TBC

As soon then as he had said unto them, I am he,
they went backward, and fell to the ground.

—JOHN 18:6

December 2

Stress can be caused by many things. You may have taken on more than you can adequately handle, you may be in a bad work situation, or there could be tensions at home. If you truly put yourself in God's hands and trust Him to guide you, He will show you what to do to relieve stressful situations to the extent that is practicable. Beyond that, stress is overcome through taking God at His Word and trusting in Him. –TBC

Thou wilt keep him in perfect peace, whose mind is stayed on thee: because he trusteth in thee.

—Isaiah 26:3

December 3

It is my understanding that we are to preach the gospel of God's grace and bring people to a saving knowledge of Christ rather than attempt to bring them under the law, however you want to describe it. I think it's a hopeless task to try to reform America, and I don't believe that task was ever given to Christians. As for paying income tax, it's my understanding from the words of Christ Himself ("Render unto Caesar the things that are Caesar's") and from His example (having Peter gather the fish with a coin in its mouth to use that coin to pay tax to the government for Peter and for Himself), as well as Romans 13, that we are to be subject to those in authority, and we are to pay custom to whom custom is due. –TBC

Render therefore to all their dues:
tribute to whom tribute is due;
custom to whom custom; fear to whom fear;
honor to whom honor.

—Romans 13:7

December 4

I have looked at the 12 Steps program closely, and have discussed it with many who are in AA. The tragedy is that AA becomes the new addiction. I have talked with people who say they are Christians and that they are trusting Christ for eternity, yet they cannot trust Him to keep them off alcohol during this life. They are desperately afraid to leave AA, because they believe it is only through AA that they can stay dry. So AA actually keeps them from the true deliverance, freedom, and joy they could know through Christ! According to AA, you are always a recovering alcoholic—never recovered. That isn't biblical. Christ cures, heals, saves, delivers. —TBC

Then Peter said, Silver and gold have I none;
but such as I have give I thee: In the name of Jesus
Christ of Nazareth rise up and walk.

—ACTS 3:6

December 5

Denounce sin publicly, seek to convict those involved of the horror of their rebellion against the God who made them, and call upon them to repent. God will bless such efforts. But don't deceive yourself into thinking you will turn America back to God if you only stage large enough demonstrations and apply enough pressure. And don't let this effort become a hindrance to, or a substitute for, preaching the gospel. –TBC

And that repentance and remission of sins
should be preached in his name among
all nations, beginning at Jerusalem.

—LUKE 24:47

December 6

Paul says that to depart [this life through death] and to be with Christ is far better than remaining alive on earth (Philippians 1:21–24). He even says that to die is gain. Certainly, that is not true if to die means to become unconscious! Revelation 6:9–10 gives a future glimpse of the souls of them that were slain in the Great Tribulation, crying out with a loud voice for God to avenge their blood. Obviously, though their bodies are dead in the grave, their souls are conscious. Numerous other scriptures testify to the same fact. –TBC

And when he had opened the fifth seal, I saw under the altar the souls of them that were slain for the word of God, and for the testimony which they held.

—Revelation 6:9

December 7

What, then, of the verses that say we must be baptized to be saved? What verses? There is not a single *one* in the Bible! Yes, Mark 16:16 says, "He that believeth and is baptized shall be saved," but that doesn't say that baptism is an essential part of salvation—only that it should *accompany* salvation. Saved people are the ones who get baptized. In fact, the rest of the verse says, "but he that believeth not shall be damned." Nowhere in the Bible does it say that he who is not baptized shall be damned; much less does it warn us that believing is not enough, by stating, "If you only believe but don't get baptized you are lost." –TBC

He that believeth and is baptized shall be saved;
but he that believeth not shall be damned.

—Mark 16:16

December 8

Serious error must be addressed and corrected. If we truly love people, then we will earnestly contend for the faith once for all delivered to the saints, and we will let them know that issues of false teaching are of eternal consequence. If Paul had held to the notion that we should not correct error for fear of embarrassing or shaming others, most of his epistles would never have been written, for they were written to address exactly the kinds of errors that many people of today want to overlook! –TBC

And others save with fear, pulling them out of the fire;
hating even the garment spotted by the flesh.

—JUDE 23

December 9

The letter kills, while the Spirit gives life. One can be as clear as crystal on doctrine and just as cold and hard in applying it to others. That fact, however, is no excuse for disregarding sound doctrine but a reminder that truth is to be spoken in love, while not compromising. Of course there are peripheral matters upon which there can be disagreement—but not when it affects the salvation of souls. Unfortunately, a false gospel is being preached today, and Paul said that those who do so are under God's curse. —TBC

Who also hath made us able ministers of the new testament; not of the letter, but of the spirit: for the letter killeth, but the spirit giveth life.

—2 CORINTHIANS 3:6

December 10

Those of us who believe in the eternal security of the believer (Christ keeps those who are truly his) are not soft on sin (as we are accused of being). We don't encourage people living in sin to believe that because they claim to have once made a decision for Christ they are secure. Much less would we offer assurance of salvation to one who has renounced his professed faith in Christ. The only difference is that we would say that such a person never was saved, while they say he lost his salvation. —TBC

What shall we say then? Shall we continue in sin, that grace may abound? God forbid. How shall we, that are dead to sin, live any longer therein?

—Romans 6:1–2

December 11

Paul solemnly swore that he would be willing to be damned eternally if that would effect the salvation of his brethren, the Jews. If God inspired such love, then surely God desires the salvation of all mankind. If God did not inspire this love, then Paul is more loving than God! And wouldn't Paul be defying God by desiring the salvation of those whom God has eternally damned? It is both biblically and logically inconsistent to say that God loves those whom He predestined to eternal doom—yet God *is* love. –TBC

For I could wish that myself were accursed from Christ for my brethren, my kinsmen according to the flesh.

—Romans 9:3

December 12

Scripture says, "The wages of sin is death" (Romans 6:23) and "the soul that sinneth, it shall die" (Ezekiel 18:4,20). Certainly death (eternal separation from God) is the penalty for sin that the law demands of each sinner. Wages are not a debt that we pile up but what we deserve for what we have done. We say that the criminal "got what he deserved." It would be accurate to say that the penalty for sin is death; and the fact that Christ "tasted death for every man" (Hebrews 2:9) could be rephrased to say that He paid the penalty for our sins. —TBC

But we see Jesus, who was made a little lower than the angels for the suffering of death, crowned with glory and honor; that he by the grace of God should taste death for every man.

—HEBREWS 2:9

December 13

The Scriptures tell us that Christ had to suffer for our sin: "Ought not Christ to have suffered these things?" (Luke 24:26); "Christ also hath once suffered for sins" (1 Peter 3:18). But how and when did He suffer? His suffering at the hands of man could not pay the penalty demanded by God's infinite justice. He was punished by the Father for our sins. As He hung on the Cross, the Father "laid on him the iniquity of us all" (Isaiah 53:6). The Bible says, "It pleased the LORD to bruise him" (Isaiah 53:10). Surely, it was the contemplation of being made sin for us—not just having nails driven into His hands and feet—that caused Him to sweat like great drops of blood in the Garden and to cry out, "If it be possible, let this cup pass from me." How could Christ, in the few hours He spent on the Cross, suffer God's eternal wrath? He is infinite. That is how. —TBC

And I said unto them, If ye think good, give me my price; and if not, forbear. So they weighed for my price thirty pieces of silver.

—ZECHARIAH 11:12

December 14

Paul declares, "the gospel which I preached…by which also ye are saved…" (1 Corinthians 15:1–4). But surely the gospel is not fully expressed there, to the Philippian jailor, to Nicodemus, the woman at the well, et al. The obvious and crucial point we must not overlook is that "believe on the Lord Jesus Christ" must of necessity include who He is. To "preach Christ" can't mean merely to say that someone called "Jesus Christ" died in our place! You cannot preach Christ without explaining who He is. In 1 Corinthians 15:1-4 the vital phrase is "according to the scriptures"—which surely includes all that the Scriptures say. How can we ask someone to believe in Jesus without explaining fully who the biblical Jesus is? —TBC

Moreover, brethren, I declare unto you the gospel which I preached unto you, which also ye have received, and wherein ye stand.

—1 Corinthians 15:1

December 15

Yes, man has freedom. God's foreknowledge has no influence at all upon the freedom to choose that God has granted to mankind. Of course He can, if it suits His purpose, influence man's action—but that is another subject. God knows every path that a person *may* take, but that has nothing to do with God's foreknowledge of what the person will actually *do*. God doesn't have to take into consideration any alternate paths. Deduction has no part in His foreknowledge. He knows the future—He knows what will happen before it happens. Time is part of the physical universe. God is outside of the universe, so He is outside of time. What to us seems past, present, and an unknown future with many possibilities is one continuum that God observes from outside time. –TBC

For the LORD knoweth the way of the righteous:
but the way of the ungodly shall perish.

—PSALM 1:6

December 16

Christians are not to be of this world. There is a real danger in entangling ourselves in the affairs of men, getting caught up in plans and programs and agendas, and thereby losing our ability to "seek those things which are above, where Christ sitteth on the right hand of God" (Colossians 3:1). The verse goes on to say, "Set your affection on things above, not on things on the earth." We are to be eagerly waiting and watching for Christ to return to take us up to be with Him forever. How sad to waste our time here on earth involved in the things that turn out to be "wood, hay, stubble..." (I Corinthians 3:10–15), yet this verse also says, "he shall suffer loss: but he himself shall be saved." –TBC

Every man's work shall be made manifest: for the day shall declare it, because it shall be revealed by fire; and the fire shall try every man's work of what sort it is.

—1 Corinthians 3:13

December 17

Regarding "taking up the cross," the primary application was to those of Christ's day. He said that they had to take up their cross. If they would be true to Him, they had to realize that they would be crucified beside Him on their own crosses. Of course, that was not possible, and they all forsook Him and fled. Today there is a different application. We are to deny self and instead are to glory in the Cross of our Lord Jesus Christ, by which the world is crucified unto us and we to the world. –TBC

And he said to them all, If any man will come after me, let him deny himself, and take up his cross daily, and follow me.

—Luke 9:23

December 18

We are required, in our love for the lost, to speak the truth. It doesn't help Muslims for us to pretend that Islam is peace. If a Muslim wants to make up his own religion, okay, but he can't call it Islam. That is an established religion with founder, scriptures, and history—and it is the opposite of peace and tolerance. You will do your Muslim friends a disservice if you avoid the truth so as not to offend. –TBC

He that speaketh truth sheweth forth righteousness: but a false witness deceit.

—PROVERBS 12:17

December 19

The evangelical church has been deluded by the value of "scholarship," which has turned them from serving the Lord to impressing men and compromising the truth in order to do so. —TBC

From which some having swerved have turned aside unto vain jangling; Desiring to be teachers of the law; understanding neither what they say, nor whereof they affirm.

—1 TIMOTHY 1:6-7

For the time will come when they will not endure sound doctrine; but after their own lusts shall they heap to themselves teachers, having itching ears.

—1 TIMOTHY 4:3

December 20

Adam never tasted the death that Christ died for him. No man has ever tasted the death that Christ died—the second death in the lake of fire for eternity. Christ had to endure that for everyone who ever lived or ever will live in order to pay the full penalty for the sin of the world. Spiritual suffering for our sins, separation from God, tasting fullness of death for every man, took place on the Cross—and nowhere else. –TBC

Who his own self bare our sins in his own body on the tree, that we, being dead to sins, should live unto righteousness: by whose stripes ye were healed.

—1 Peter 2:24

December 21

The very power of choice that enables us to receive Christ by faith is itself God's sovereign gift—and receiving a gift gives no reason to boast. Calvinists say that free will would "limit God's freedom." *They* limit God! If God cannot exercise His sovereignty unhindered by man's free will, He is limited indeed. –TBC

For if by one man's offence death reigned by one; much more they which receive abundance of grace and of the gift of righteousness shall reign in life by one, Jesus Christ.

—Romans 5:17

December 22

Do I know that I am saved because I am living a good enough life? It is true that John writes, "He that saith he abideth in him ought himself also so to walk, even as he walked" (I John 2:6). That is the standard—but who would dare to say that he walks as Christ walked? We are not to sin, but at times we do; indeed, we deceive ourselves if we deny that. But Christ never sinned, so how can a sinner be said to walk as Christ walked? Assurance doesn't come by the life I live, for then I could not have any assurance upon receiving Christ but only after I had lived for Him long enough to "prove" that I was a real Christian. Paul says that one who doesn't have even one good work is yet truly saved if he believes on Christ. John 5:24 says of those who believe, that they have "passed from death unto life." This happens at the moment of believing on Christ. –TBC

He that believeth on the Son hath everlasting life: and he that believeth not the Son shall not see life; but the wrath of God abideth on him.

—JOHN 3:36

December 23

The Lord sent an evil spirit to Saul to test him, and he failed the test. Jesus was "led up of the Spirit…to be tempted of the devil" (Matthew 4:1). There are tests and trials in our lives that are designed for "the trial of your faith, being much more precious than of gold that perisheth, though it be tried with fire, [that it] might be found unto praise and honour and glory at the appearing of Jesus Christ…" (1 Peter 1:7). Greet each bout of "depression" with joy: another opportunity for your faith to grow, for you to triumph in Christ! –TBC

Rejoice in the Lord alway: and again I say, Rejoice.

—Philippians 4:4

December 24

Each trial that we experience is another opportunity to trust the Lord in order to bring glory to Him. How it grieves Him for us to doubt: "O ye of little faith" (Matthew 6:25–34); "Trust in the LORD with all thine heart; and lean not unto thine own understanding…he will direct thy paths" (Proverbs 3:5–6). –TBC

…this day is holy unto our Lord: neither be ye sorry;
for the joy of the LORD is your strength.

—NEHEMIAH 8:10

December 25

Ultimately, when you stand before the Lord face to face, He will not ask what someone else told you but will hold you accountable for what you yourself believe. Continue without striving or panic but with quiet trust to seek the Lord about matters that trouble you until you are deeply satisfied with His answer. He's the One from whom perfect answers come. —TBC

But why dost thou judge thy brother?
or why dost thou set at nought thy brother?
for we shall all stand before the judgment seat of Christ.

—Romans 14:10

December 26

We are all needy people—needing our Lord's mercy and each other's fellowship and encouragement. When such fellowship is lacking, it is an affront to the Savior who made us one. It is an affront to our brothers and sisters for whom Christ died. It is a loss to us when we are deprived (or deprive ourselves) of such brotherly ties. It is also a disgrace before the eyes of the world to represent our Lord so poorly. And yet, in so many churches today, the need for fellowship is not met and many go hungry for want of true friendships in the Body. A practical word—fervently seek always and everywhere to be that "angel unawares" yourself. This is joy! —TBC

Not forsaking the assembling of ourselves together,
as the manner of some is; but exhorting one another:
and so much the more, as ye see the day approaching.

—HEBREWS 10:25

December 27

Proverbs 3:5–6 tells us to "Trust in the LORD with all thine heart; and lean not unto thine own understanding. In all thy ways acknowledge him, and he shall direct thy paths." The sense of this passage would indicate that we are active participants in the discovery of the Lord's will. In other words, we are not sitting—waiting for the Lord to steer us before we move. May you be encouraged to go forward in confidence, knowing that the Lord's sure direction will guide you. –TBC

The steps of a good man are ordered by the LORD: and he delighteth in his way.

—PSALM 37:23

December 28

Tithing was a law for the Israelites but not for Christians, who are not under the Law but Grace. Nevertheless, some Christians choose to tithe as a form for their giving to the Lord's work. As Christians, everything we have is the Lord's; therefore, we give as the Lord leads, with a cheerful heart—not on the basis of Law. To use the tithe as a basis of giving is fine, as long as it is a matter of the heart; however, there are many misunderstandings in the Body of Christ about this subject. For instance, people who tithe can give for the wrong reasons (to fulfill an obligation instead of from a loving response); and they might think they've done all they should do, when the Lord may want them to do much more. –TBC

Every man according as he purposeth in his heart, so let him give; not grudgingly, or of necessity: for God loveth a cheerful giver.

—2 Corinthians 9:7

December 29

Jesus' "cursing" of the fig tree is not an indication that the Lord was having some sort of temper tantrum brought on by His hunger. "Cursing" in this case did not involve the use of profanity but was simply a pronouncement against the tree. Throughout Scripture, the fig tree is used as a type of Israel. Consequently, a fruitless fig tree being cursed by the Lord—Israel's Messiah and prophesied King—would have great meaning to Christ's Jewish disciples. And although they have been temporarily set aside, as Paul points out in Romans 11:1–26, they have certainly not been cast away. –TBC

For the Jews require a sign,
and the Greeks seek after wisdom…

—1 Corinthians 1:22

December 30

One might learn from the experience of the man who had a heart after God (David) and yet still gave in to adultery and murder, with horrible results for his family. No wonder that I Corinthians 10:6–7, speaking of the Old Testament experience of the Israelites, very plainly tells us that "these things were our examples, to the intent we should not lust after evil things, as they also lusted." Other passages indicate that the entire experience of Israel (including their kings) was recorded so that we might learn and avoid the same errors and sins. –TBC

Now all these things happened unto them for ensamples: and they are written for our admonition, upon whom the ends of the world are come.

—1 Corinthians 10:11

December 31

New heresies (as well as recycled old ones) and false teachings and false teachers continue to appear on the scene all the time, and being a Berean (measuring everything by the Scriptures) can protect the believer from falling prey to these even before they are identified by some name or description. It is absolutely imperative today, we believe, to be a Berean and to develop discernment as an individual. Continue to seek God. That is our heart's cry and calling here at The Berean Call: that we would see people developing personal discernment and, like the Bereans in Acts 17:11, searching the Scriptures daily to see if these things were so. Ultimately, each must arrive at his own position, for each is accountable to God for what he believes, not for what someone else proclaimed or taught. –TBC

These were more noble than those in Thessalonica, in that they received the word with all readiness of mind, and searched the scriptures daily, whether those things were so.

—ACTS 17:11

A word fitly spoken is like apples of gold in pictures of silver. —Proverbs 25:11

You might also enjoy:

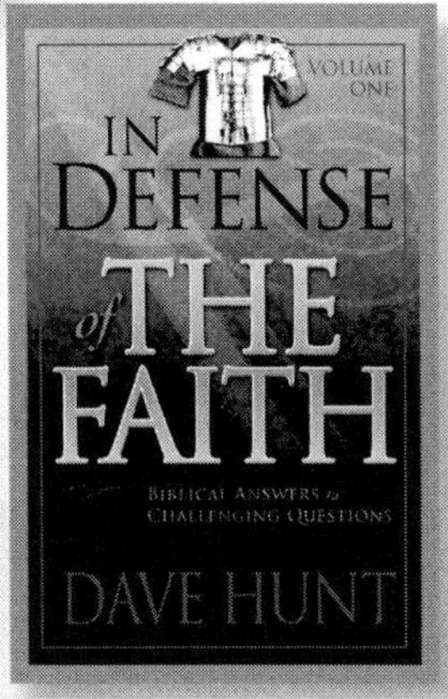

IN DEFENSE OF THE FAITH: Biblical Answers to Challenging Questions

By Dave Hunt—When confronted with uncomfortable questions from atheists and agnostics, cultists and pagans, or skeptics and mystics, do your once-firm convictions begin to crumble and compromise? Do you tend to take flight—or instead, are you able to stand firm and "earnestly contend for the faith"? With the keen eye of an experienced treasure hunter, the author helps readers probe and unearth the incredible wealth of guidance found in God's Word. The resulting adventure will not only strengthen the faith of believers but equip them to live daily according to His revealed truth in an increasingly hostile world. This fascinating book provides biblical answers to many of life's most challenging questions:

Is There a Difference Between Faith and Belief? • Is It Wrong to Want Evidence of God? • How Do We Deal with Doubts? • If We Can Prove God Exists, Why Faith? • Why Do Christians Accept Only One God? • Who Is the True God? • Can We Know God? • Are God and Nature the Same? • Is It Wrong to Ask God to Reveal Himself? • Is Jesus Half-God & Half-Man? • Is the Bible Reliable? • Is the Bible the Only Book of God? • Were Biblical Prophecies Written After the Events? • Shouldn't We Examine All Religions? • Can the Bible Be Verified? • How Do We Know Our Copies of the Bible Are Accurate? • Can You Make the Bible Say Anything You Want? • Is the Bible Infallible? • Do the Gospels Disagree?

BONUS MP3: Included with the book is a one-disc MP3 radio discussion of *In Defense of the Faith.* Recorded for radio broadcast, this archival series spans nearly 100 segments (about 23 minutes each) that comprise nearly 37 hours of fascinating discussion.

ISBN 978-1-928660-66-8 • The Berean Call • paperback, 373 pages

ABOUT THE BEREAN CALL

The Berean Call (TBC) is a non-denominational, tax-exempt organization which exists to:

ALERT believers in Christ to unbiblical teachings and practices impacting the church

EXHORT believers to give greater heed to biblical discernment and truth regarding teachings and practices being currently promoted in the church

SUPPLY believers with teaching, information, and materials which will encourage the love of God's truth, and assist in the development of biblical discernment

MOBILIZE believers in Christ to action in obedience to the scriptural command to "earnestly contend for the faith" (Jude 3)

IMPACT the church of Jesus Christ with the necessity for trusting the Scriptures as the only rule for faith, practice, and a life pleasing to God

A free monthly newsletter, THE BEREAN CALL, may be received by sending a request to: PO Box 7019, Bend, OR 97708; or by calling

1-800-937-6638

To register for free email updates, to access our digital archives, and to order a variety of additional resource materials online, visit us at:

www.thebereancall.org

Also by Dave Hunt:

WHATEVER HAPPENED TO HEAVEN?
(From the "Dave Hunt Classic" Series)

By Dave Hunt—More than two decades after the original printing of this book, yet another bible prophecy is proving itself true today:

> *There shall come in the last days scoffers, walking after their own [desires] . . . saying, "Where is the promise of his coming? for since the fathers fell asleep, all things continue as they were from the beginning of the creation"* (2 Peter 3:3-4).

During the 1970s when *The Late, Great Planet Earth* was outselling everything, the rapture was the hot topic. Pastors preached about heaven, and Christians eagerly anticipated being taken up at any moment to meet their Lord in the air. When Christ didn't return and the 40 years since the establishment of a new Israel in 1948 expired without the fulfillment of prophesied events, disillusionment began to set in.

Today, a growing number of Christians are exchanging the hope for the rapture for a "new" hope . . . that Christians can clean up society and elect enough of their own candidates to political office to make this world a "heaven on earth."

Bestselling author Dave Hunt probes that question thoroughly and provides an easily understandable explanation of all the many issues and beliefs. Hunt shows us that a literal heaven really *is* our home —and brings fascinating new clarity to how we lost that hope and how it can be regained.

ISBN 978-1-928660-70-5 • The Berean Call • paperback, 327 pages

You might also enjoy:

YOGA AND THE BODY OF CHRIST:
What Position Should Christians Hold?

By Dave Hunt—That non-Christians are engaging in yoga is not surprising. After all, it is being promoted in the West as purely physical stretching and breathing exercises beneficial for one's health—even as a cure for cancer, with testimonials that supposedly back up that claim. That Christians, however, who say they follow Christ and His Word, would also jump on the bandwagon of Eastern mysticism is staggering.

Yoga was developed to escape this "unreal" world of time and sense and to reach moksha, the Hindu heaven—or to return to the "void" of the Buddhist. With its breathing exercises and limbering-up positions, yoga is promoted in the West for enhancing health and better living—but in the far East, where it originated, it is understood to be a way of dying.

Promising to bring peace, healing, and wholeness (even prosperity!) to its practitioners, readers will be shocked to discover that yoga is, in fact, based on the worship of (and prepares participants for supernatural connection with) unholy spirits that manifest in extraordinary and dangerous ways. The author—an avid promoter of biblically based physical, mental, and spiritual wholeness—distinguishes pure truth from popular belief in this revealing expose. Every Christian should be informed of the true origins and effects of the practice of yoga and its ungodly roots in Kundalini energy—which, literally defined, means an awakening of the "Serpent Power."

Chapters: • What About Yoga? • Yoga for Christians? • The Aquarian Conspiracy • The Conquest of the West • Beware the "Science" of Yoga • "The Great Dragon...That Old Serpent" • Yoga's Kundalini Serpent Power • Yoga, Reincarnation, and Truth

ISBN 978-1-928660-48-4 • The Berean Call • paperback, 175 pages

Also by Dave Hunt:

SEEKING AND FINDING GOD:
In Search of the True Faith

By Dave Hunt—It is astonishing how many millions of otherwise seemingly intelligent people are willing to risk their eternal destiny upon less evidence than they would require for buying a car or even a low-carb food item—yet the belief of so many, particularly in the area of religion, has no rational or factual foundation.

With well-researched arguments and compelling proof, this book demonstrates that the issue of where one will spend eternity is not a matter of preference (like joining the Elks instead of the Lions).

In fact, there is overwhelming evidence that we are eternal beings who will spend eternity somewhere.

But where will it be?

And how can we know?

There is no more important question to be faced—and answered.

Chapters:

- The Necessity of Certainty • Of God and Human Destiny • Of Bodies and Spirits
- In Search of the True Faith • Concerning Prayer • Shortcut to Truth
- What is the Gospel? • Mercy vs. Works • The Call to Discipleship

ISBN 978-1-928660-23-1 • The Berean Call • paperback, 159 pages